THE ANXIOUS GENERATION CURE

A Calming Guide for Panicked Parents: Become the Regulated Adult Who Raises Regulated Children

Madeline Armstrong

We believe in the power of shared knowledge.

But we also respect the time and effort invested here.

So please, honor this work.

PREFACE

I know why you picked up this book.

Because you are tired of the noise.

Tired of the anxiety that feels thick in the air.

It's not just your children who are panicking.

It is you.

It is me.

We are living in a time of high alert.

Maybe you feel like you are failing.

Maybe you've read all the other books.

And they left you feeling guilty or inadequate.

That stops here.

This is not a manual filled with impossible rules.

This is a quiet, steady conversation.

It is about moving from fear to presence.

It is about understanding the simple, elegant science that governs all human behavior.

We are going to start with you.

We are going to regulate the adult first.

Because a regulated adult is the greatest gift we can give to a child.

Ready to breathe?

TABLE OF CONTENTS

INTRODUCTION

THE SHOCKING TRUTH ABOUT WHY YOUR "GENTLE PARENTING" MANUAL KEEPS FAILING (AND HOW TO FIX IT INSTANTLY)

There is a chaos happening right now.

It hums beneath the surface of every family dinner.

It flares up during every screen time argument.

Every transition feels like a battlefield.

We call it 'the anxious generation'.

But let's be honest.

It's the anxious parents raising the anxious generation.

Right?

We are exhausted. We are overwhelmed. We feel perpetually inadequate. The market is saturated with "gentle parenting" guides and "conscious discipline" courses. We read them. We memorize the scripts. We tell ourselves, I will be patient. I will validate their feelings.

Then Tuesday afternoon hits.

The backpack is thrown. The homework is refused. The sibling is punched. The noise escalates. And suddenly, your carefully constructed parenting strategy dissolves. You hear the yell escaping your throat. You feel the sharp, cold disconnection of withdrawal.

It felt like a tidal wave hit us.

We try to be patient. We try to be gentle. We try to be connected. Then our own nervous system screams. Our physiological threat detector goes off. We revert to primal reactions. We resort to yelling. Or threatening. Or withdrawing. And then the crippling, suffocating guilt crashes in.

I know that cycle intimately. I lived it. I coached thousands of parents through it.

The shocking truth is this: those parenting manuals—the ones that talk only about what to say to your child—they fail because they skip the most critical step. They skip the prerequisite. They assume you, the adult, are already calm. They assume you are regulated.

You are not. None of us are, consistently.

This book is your exit ramp. It is not another script to memorize. It is built on a simple premise that changes everything: We must heal the nervous system before we can heal the home.

We are not dealing with a behavior problem. We are dealing with a biological problem.

We are going to blend hard neuroscience—the elegant, simple science of safety—with profound, non-judgmental empathy. We are going to look at why things happen inside your body. Not just what to do when they happen outside your child's body.

You already have the love. You already have the intention. What you are missing are the biological tools to stay present when the pressure is on.

We are shifting the focus entirely. Less focus on controlling the child. More focus on steadying the adult.

Because a child's behaviour is always, always, a reflection of their internal state. And their internal state is always mirroring the safety signal—or lack thereof—coming from their primary caregiver. You are their safety anchor. You must be steady.

This is a journey toward becoming the safe haven your children desperately need. The calm you cultivate within yourself will become the calm they breathe in your home.

Let's begin the essential work of coming home to ourselves.

CHAPTER ONE

—★-★-★—

THE PARENT TRAP: EXPOSED: WHY YOUR CONSTANT WORRY IS THE #1 SABOTEUR OF YOUR CHILD'S STABILITY

THIS CONSTANT HUM OF DREAD. DO YOU FEEL IT?

It's the invisible third parent in every home right now. We call it "parental worry." But worry is too gentle a word. This is chronic, low-grade panic. It sits in your shoulders. It tightens your chest when the school phone rings. It screams inside your head: Am I doing enough? Is my child safe?

We are wired for concern. Concern is good. Concern makes you buckle the seatbelt. Concern helps you set boundaries. Concern is proactive, grounded, and temporary. It gets a job done.

What we are dealing with today is fundamentally different. It is free-floating anxiety. It has no object. It's an alarm system stuck permanently on the "high alert" setting. It's exhausting. It's draining. And it is the single biggest impediment to your child's well-being.

Understand this deeply: Your nervous system is the climate of your home.

When you are walking around constantly activated—waiting for the next crisis, scrolling for the next danger, or beating yourself up over the last failure—you are projecting instability. You are transmitting stress.

Children are expert emotional radar detectors. They don't hear the gentle words you use when you are panicking. They feel the frequency of your fear. They feel the tension in your jaw. They absorb the quick, short breaths you take when you think you are hiding your stress.

They learn to regulate, or dysregulate, based on your steady presence.

If the adult container is shaky, the child cannot trust the space. If the adult is constantly in fight-or-flight mode, the child assumes the world must be dangerous.

We've tried every discipline method. We've read the scripts. We've built the sticker charts. None of it works if we start from a place of internal chaos.

The trap is believing you must fix the child first.

The truth is, you must regulate the adult first.

This book is dedicated to helping you become the regulated adult. The steady anchor. The calm, warm center of the storm.

We are not going to stop caring about our kids. We are going to stop letting fear run the show. We are going to reclaim our calm. We are going to learn how to lend our stability to our children instead of lending them our anxiety.

That transition—from anxious reactor to steady regulator—is the greatest gift you can offer. It changes everything.

—★-★-★—

THE "10-SECOND NEWS CYCLE" OVERLOAD: HOW MODERN LIFE ZAPS YOUR INTERNAL BATTERY (AND THE 1-MINUTE REBOOT)

We are soaked in noise.

The news cycle used to be once a day. Now it is continuous. It's relentless. A million pieces of data hit your brain before your first cup of coffee.

A headline flashes. A siren wails outside. Your feed shows a perfect stranger achieving a perfect milestone.

Your brain processes all of it the same way. It is stimulus. It is input. It is danger.

Your nervous system is designed to keep you alive. When it sees constant input—even if it's just digital—it assumes there is a threat lurking nearby. It keeps the alert system on HIGH.

You are running on chronic vigilance.

Adrenaline trickles instead of rushing. Cortisol pools instead of dissipating. You become hyper-vigilant. Irritable. Quick to snap.

This is the state we call "tired."

But it is not simple fatigue. It is a deep, biological depletion. Your internal battery is always seeking a charge, but you keep plugging it into chaos.

Then your child does something perfectly normal—maybe they cry, maybe they whine—and your already maxed-out system treats that sound like the final alarm bell.

You jump from zero to one hundred instantly. Why? Because you were never at zero to begin with. You were perpetually at sixty.

Chronic vigilance is the enemy of patience. You cannot possibly be steady when your internal landscape is constantly vibrating with unseen dread.

This stops now.

We need a hard reset. A moment to drop the digital weight and return to the physical world.

The 1-Minute Reboot is your power switch.

First, identify the digital source that is feeding the frenzy. The phone. The laptop. The television screen. Step away from it. Physically. Put it in another room.

Second, engage your senses. Look around the room you are in. Name five things you see. Slowly. Out loud or whispered.

Third, take one deep, audible sigh. Not a breath in. A breath out. Let the sound carry away the tension.

You have just signalled to your Vagus nerve: I am safe. The threat is not here.

One minute. That is all the time needed to break the cycle of high alert and reclaim the present moment. Do this often. Interrupt the constant feed. Give your system a genuine moment of rest. Recharge the battery before the next interaction.

Your peace is your children's stability. Protect it fiercely.

WARNING: THE GUILT-SHAME LOOP THAT KEEPS YOU STUCK (AND THE 3 STEPS TO YOUR EMOTIONAL PERMISSION SLIP)

YOU KNOW THE FEELING.

It's the silent, toxic residue left over after a moment of parental failure. Maybe you yelled about the spilled milk. Maybe you gave the silent treatment when they resisted bedtime. The incident is over, but the echo remains. That deep, visceral conviction: I am failing them.

This is not helpful regret. This is the guilt-shame loop.

Guilt says, "I did something wrong." Guilt is useful. It guides you toward making amends. Shame says, "I am wrong." Shame is paralyzing. It is highly dysregulating, and when you are flooded with shame, your nervous system slams the door shut. You cannot connect, you cannot repair, and you definitely cannot regulate your child when you are frozen in self-judgment.

We treat this shame like motivation. We think if we beat ourselves up enough, we'll do better next time. We won't. Shame only teaches you one thing: to hide.

The most compassionate, powerful thing you can do for your children is to free yourself from this loop. You must grant yourself an emotional permission slip to be imperfect.

Here are the three steps to ripping up that permission slip:

1. THE WITNESS MOMENT: NAME THE EMOTION WITHOUT JUDGMENT

Stop trying to reason your way out of the feeling. Just name the sensation. When that hot, prickly feeling of failure rises, do not immediately try to fix the situation or yourself. Simply observe: Ah. This is shame. I feel tight in my chest. I hear that old script running. By naming it, you create space between you and the emotion. You become the witness, not the victim. This 10-second action halts the immediate spiral.

2. ACKNOWLEDGE THE BIOLOGICAL TRIGGER

Remind yourself that your reaction—the yelling, the snapping, the withdrawing—was not a moral failing. It was a nervous system response. It was your brain's ancient wiring perceiving a threat (the chaos, the defiance, the fatigue) and throwing you into a defensive state. Say this to yourself: My reaction was rooted in exhaustion, not malice. My adult brain was hijacked. My system went into overload. This de-personalizes the fault and allows your higher brain to come back online. You forgive the system so the self can heal.

3. PRIORITIZE RADICAL SELF-COMPASSION AND IMMEDIATE REPAIR

Your highest duty after a mistake is not self-flagellation; it is repair. You cannot repair with your child until you repair with yourself. Give yourself the kindness you would offer a best friend in the same situation. Use the emotional permission slip: I give myself permission to be a human being, which means I will make mistakes. I accept this as part of my humanity, and I will now turn my focus outward. This isn't about ignoring the incident. It's about not wasting valuable regulation energy on pointless, punitive shame. Take one deep breath, find your feet on the floor, and immediately pivot toward your child to re-establish connection. This is the only way out of the loop.

—★-★-★—

THE SINGLE BIOLOGICAL PREREQUISITE YOUR CHILD NEEDS MORE THAN DISCIPLINE (HINT: IT'S NOT LOVE)

We talk constantly about love. We believe love is the answer to everything. It is essential, yes. But biologically, love is not enough.

The single, non-negotiable prerequisite your child needs is a pervasive, felt sense of safety.

Your child's nervous system is the most ancient, sophisticated security system ever devised. Its sole, non-stop function is survival. It is constantly scanning the environment—the sound of your voice, the tension in your shoulders, the speed of your movements—to answer one critical question: Am I safe here?

If the answer is anything less than a resounding Yes, the system overrides all other functions.

It doesn't care about compliance. It doesn't care about chores. It doesn't care that they just threw their sandwich across the room.

If the nervous system registers danger—and remember, parental frustration or yelling registers as a profound social threat—the sophisticated part of the brain that manages cooperation, planning, and emotional regulation instantly goes offline.

You cannot successfully discipline or teach a child who is operating from a state of biological defense. You are lecturing a survival mechanism. It will not listen.

This is the key distinction we miss: Discipline and effective communication only become possible once the child's nervous system is regulated.

Regulation comes first. Safety is the foundation. Everything else is built upon that quiet, internal steadiness. Our work, therefore, begins with creating that safety, starting with the safest place of all: the parent's own calm.

—★–★–★—

THE SILENT PROTOCOL THAT INSTANTLY HALTS PANIC ATTACKS WHEN YOUR KID BLOWS UP

YOUR CHILD IS MELTING DOWN. THE VOLUME IS DEAFENING. THE AIR feels electric and charged.

Your first biological instinct is panic. It screams: Intervene! Fix this! Make the noise stop! Your sympathetic nervous system is screaming at you to react. Your chest tightens. You feel the familiar, sickening pressure of failure.

This is where you execute the Silent Protocol.

It is simple. It is radical. It is the single most effective tool you will learn.

The protocol is this: When chaos erupts, your first responsibility is not to your child's behavior. It is to your own body.

You have explicit permission, right now, to stop the action and regulate yourself. Before you say a word. Before you move toward them. Before you try to soothe, correct, or distract.

You are allowed to pause. You are required to pause.

You must become the safe container before you can put the contents inside. A regulated adult is the greatest possible resource for a dysregulated child. If you are spiking, they will only spike harder. If you are panicking, you are co-panicking.

Stop trying to hold up the house while standing on Jell-O.

The Silent Protocol is the moment you inwardly declare: I am prioritizing my own steady breathing. I am putting my feet firmly on the floor. I am dropping my shoulders. I am allowing the panic to pass through me before I open my mouth.

This is not selfish. This is essential parenting.

It grants you the necessary distance to observe the situation rather than drown in the emotion. It gives you the power to choose connection over control.

Take a deep breath. Let it out. You do not have to fix them instantly. You only have to steady yourself first. This is the exit ramp from the anxiety loop. This is your relief.

CHAPTER TWO

—★–★–★—

THE HIDDEN WIRING DIAGRAM: DECODING YOUR OWN BRAIN'S REACTION BEFORE YOU EVER TALK TO YOUR KID

THE HARDEST PART ABOUT WANTING TO BE A CALM PARENT IS HOW quickly you lose that ability the moment a challenge arises.

You read the books. You meditate. You promise yourself you will use your soft voice.

Then the juice spills. The sibling fight escalates. Your teenager gives you that silent, disrespectful glare.

And suddenly, a different person answers. This person yells. This person slams a door. This person withdraws into complete silence, ignoring the chaos entirely.

Who is that person?

It's not the person you want to be. It's the person wired for survival.

Until now, you likely viewed that reaction as a character flaw, a failure of willpower. We tend to moralize our physiological responses: "I should be more patient." "I am a bad parent because I yelled."

We need to flip the script. Your reaction is not a moral failing. It is a biological imperative running on outdated software.

Your body is not built for the nuances of modern gentle parenting. It is built for avoiding saber-toothed tigers.

We must understand this biological fact if we ever want lasting change. We must become fluent in our own nervous system's language.

Neuroscience calls this crucial understanding Polyvagal Theory (PVT). You don't need a PhD to master it. You just need to understand three core safety states that govern every single interaction you have with your child.

Think of your nervous system as your body's constant, invisible security guard. This guard is always scanning the environment, deciding one thing: Am I safe enough to connect, or do I need to defend?

When your child is defiant or upset, your internal security guard doesn't see a toddler struggling with big feelings. It sees a threat to the stability of the tribe. It sees danger. And it deploys one of its three emergency protocols.

If you don't read the hidden wiring diagram of your own brain, you will always be reactive. You will always be driven by fear, not intention.

This chapter is your key. It reveals the map of your inner life. When you know where you are on the map—what state you are operating from —you can choose your destination. You can choose calm.

The goal is simple: Before you ever speak to your child, you must first read your own physiological state. You must regulate the adult. Because a triggered parent cannot possibly soothe a triggered child.

Let's turn on the lights and look at the wiring.

REVEALED: THE "BRAKE PEDAL" HIDING IN YOUR CHEST THAT STOPS PARENTAL MELTDOWNS DEAD IN THEIR TRACKS

You know the feeling. The heat rising in your neck. The tight knot in your stomach. That is your system flooring the gas pedal. Your stress response is kicking in. You feel out of control.

What if I told you there is a reliable brake pedal? It is built into your body. It is always there.

It is called the Vagus nerve. (Pronounced Vay-gus).

It is the longest nerve in the human body. Think of it as a massive, two-way highway. It starts in the brain stem. It runs down through your throat and chest. It connects to your heart, lungs, and gut.

This nerve is your master regulator. It is the core mechanism of the Parasympathetic Nervous System. That is the system responsible for "rest and digest."

The Vagus nerve is constantly taking readings. It assesses the safety of your environment. Is the room calm? Is the noise level acceptable? Is the face of the person looking at me friendly?

If the Vagus nerve detects safety, it sends the calming signal. It tells your heart to slow down. It tells your breath to deepen. It tells your muscles to relax.

When you are triggered by a screaming child, the Vagus nerve is momentarily suppressed. Your "fight or flight" mechanism takes over.

Our job as regulated parents is to intentionally tap this brake. We must reactivate the Vagus nerve. We override the automatic panic.

When you learn to stimulate this nerve, you create immediate physiological calm. You stop the internal meltdown dead in its tracks. You become instantly present. You access your wisdom.

The wisdom is not in your brain. It is in the regulated flow between your brain and your body. The Vagus nerve is the connection point. Learn to use it, and you possess the ultimate parenting tool. This is the physiological prerequisite for every successful interaction.

THE 3 PHYSIOLOGICAL TRAPS THAT TURN YOU INTO THE PARENT YOU SWORE YOU'D NEVER BE (IDENTIFY YOURS NOW)

We have to stop thinking of parental reaction as a conscious moral failure. It is not. It is ancient biology taking over. When the pressure cooker explodes—when the kid throws the food, when the teenager rolls their eyes—your nervous system instantly picks one of three defensive strategies.

These are the three physiological traps that hijack your prefrontal cortex, bypass your gentle parenting manual, and turn you into the reactive person you swore you'd never become.

Your first job is simply to identify which trap is your default.

TRAP 1: THE FIGHT RESPONSE (THE ROAR)

This is pure sympathetic activation. Your internal safety alarm has decided the quickest way out of this chaos is through dominance and control.

How it manifests in parenting:

You yell. Immediately.

Your voice becomes sharp, high, and demanding.

You might feel physical heat, a flushed face, or clenched jaw.

You start finger-pointing or using harsh, punitive language.

You feel an intense need for the child to submit immediately.

You are attempting to control the environment by overpowering the perceived threat (the child's defiance).

If you are a parent who struggles with a quick temper or feeling intensely angry and demanding immediate compliance, this is your biological default.

TRAP 2: THE FLIGHT RESPONSE (THE ESCAPE)

THIS RESPONSE IS ALSO DRIVEN BY SYMPATHETIC ENERGY, BUT INstead of confronting the threat, the system seeks rapid distance. The overwhelming anxiety makes the environment feel toxic.

How it manifests in parenting:

You physically retreat, slamming the door, or storming off to a different room.

You excessively worry, becoming the 'helicopter parent' who constantly plans, schedules, and micromanages to pre-emptively stop bad things from happening.

You avoid necessary conflict, giving in too easily just to restore quiet.

You feel anxious, tight-chested, and panicked about the future (Are they going to fail? Is this behaviour permanent?).

You are trying to escape the emotional intensity of the present moment.

If you are a parent who feels constantly stressed, overwhelmed, and wishes you could just hide until the age of 18, this is likely your biological default.

TRAP 3: THE FREEZE RESPONSE (THE SHUTDOWN)

THIS IS THE MOST MISUNDERSTOOD TRAP. IT IS A FULL DORSAL VAGAL brake—a total conservation of energy. Your system believes confrontation or escape is impossible, so it chooses to play dead.

How it manifests in parenting:

You go silent. You stare blankly.

Your body feels heavy, numb, or paralyzed. You literally cannot move to intervene.

You emotionally check out during a meltdown, maybe reaching for your phone or zoning out in front of the TV while chaos reigns around you.

You feel utterly helpless and hopeless.

Your voice becomes monotone or disappears entirely. You have nothing left to give.

If you are a parent who experiences periods of profound numbness, paralysis during conflict, or finds yourself withdrawing completely when the kids get loud, this is your biological default.

Understanding your primary trap is the pivot point. It is the moment you stop blaming yourself for "failing to be patient" and start seeing your reaction as a predictable, biological event. This event can be managed.

What is your trap? Name it. Write it down. This awareness is your first step toward regulation.

—★-★-★—

HOW TO FIND YOUR INNER OASIS: A 60-SECOND TECHNIQUE TO GROUND YOURSELF DURING TOTAL FAMILY CHAOS

When the crisis erupts—a child screaming, a defiant look, a sudden spike of anxiety—your nervous system instantly wants to find an external solution or an external escape. But the fastest route to calm is usually not through the environment; it is straight back to your own inner landscape. We need to install an anchor point, a place of safety you can access regardless of the storm outside.

This is a sixty-second inner resource exercise.

First, stop trying to fix the external problem for a single moment. Allow yourself three intentional, deep breaths. Close your eyes, even if just for a blink.

Now, instead of focusing on the noise, I want you to shift your attention inward and locate a moment, any moment, when you felt profoundly safe, steady, and secure. This doesn't have to be a major life event. It might be the feel of a warm blanket, a quiet morning before dawn, or the smell of rain. Access the memory that signifies true, unconditional ease.

Do not stop at the memory itself. Go deeper.

When you recall that feeling of security, where does it live in your body? That feeling of peace always has a physical signature. Focus on locating it now.

Does your chest feel open, expansive, and warm? That sensation is your anchor.

Do you feel a deep, heavy weight in your hips and feet, a feeling of being absolutely grounded to the floor? That stability is your resource.

Is there a soft, quiet space behind your ribcage, a place where the tension seems to dissolve? Breathe into that space.

Your inner oasis is that physical spot where genuine calm resides. It might be a warmth in your belly, a relaxed jaw, or a sense of spaciousness around your heart. This is not manufactured calm; this is retrieved safety.

The moment chaos hits, you will stop the immediate reaction and instantly cue your mind to find that physical signature. Instead of saying, "I must control this child," you mentally say, "I must locate the softness in my chest."

Breathe once, aiming your attention directly at that physical anchor point for sixty seconds. You are literally borrowing that feeling of regulation from your resource memory and lending it to your current, activated self. You are creating a portable, internal island of safety that no external tantrum can ever breach. Use this sensory connection to the self as the foundation for your next interaction.

—— ★-★-★ ——

DISCOVERED: THE 5 'INVISIBLE' MICRO-MOMENTS YOU MUST WEAVE INTO YOUR DAY TO STAY UNSHAKABLE

We often sabotage our own regulation attempts by designing routines that require thirty minutes of uninterrupted solitude. If you are a parent, you know this is fantasy.

Regulation is not about overhauls. It is about consistent, tiny micro-doses of safety. These five micro-moments are the invisible armor you can weave into the fabric of your busiest day. They are simple acts that signal to your vagus nerve: "I am safe. I have time."

1. THE COLD SIP RESET

Keep a glass of ice water nearby. When you feel a spike of frustration—the kind that makes your shoulders tighten—take a slow, purposeful sip of the cold water. The sudden shift in temperature in your mouth and throat briefly stimulates the vagus nerve. It's an instant, internal shock that forces a physiological pause. Use it after hanging up a tense phone call or before starting the dishes. It takes two seconds. It works.

2. THE AUDITORY HUM

The vagus nerve passes near the vocal cords. Low-frequency vibration is deeply soothing. When you are standing in line, waiting for the microwave, or sitting in traffic, simply hum. A deep, low "mmmmmm" that you feel slightly vibrating in your chest. You don't have to make noise;

you can do it with your lips closed. This gentle toning of the vagal nerve sends a direct message of calm from your throat to your brain.

3. THE 5-SECOND HORIZON

Modern life keeps us focused on screens, laundry piles, and small, immediate problems. This keeps our nervous system hyper-focused and activated. Several times a day, look up. Look far away. Look out a window or down the hallway to the farthest point you can see. Hold that gaze for five seconds. This broadens your visual field, signalling to your ancient brain that the immediate threat (the one right in front of your face) is not all that exists. It's a literal change in perspective.

4. THE FOOT-ON-THE-FLOOR ANCHOR

Every time you sit down, before you do anything else, intentionally press both feet firmly into the floor. Feel the ground beneath you. Notice the texture, the pressure, the solidity. Anxiety pulls us out of our bodies and into our minds. Grounding pulls us back down. If you are sitting while reading this, do it now. Press your feet down. This is an immediate, stabilizing sensory anchor you can use 50 times a day.

5. THE WRIST RUB PROTOCOL

Deep, slow, intentional pressure is a powerful form of self-soothing. When you are brushing your teeth, waiting for the kettle to boil, or simply walking, slowly rub the inside of one wrist with two fingers of the opposite hand. This is a subtle self-touch that is calming and easy to conceal. It's a way of saying, "I'm here with you," to your own body. It's the physical, soothing presence you often give your child, but directed inward.

The key to these micro-moments is to attach them to actions you already perform. They are not one more thing to remember; they are a subtle shift in the way you inhabit your body during the moments that already exist. Consistency, even in two-second intervals, changes the baseline of your nervous system.

CHAPTER THREE

THE ART OF THE PAUSE: THE INSTANT SELF-CONTROL MECHANISM THAT MOVES YOU FROM YELLING TO WISDOM IN 3 SECONDS FLAT

THE TRIGGER HITS.

It is fast.

It is a flash of heat in your chest.

It is the sudden grip in your jaw.

Your child just tossed the juice.

They screamed "No" one too many times.

The nervous system doesn't wait for permission.

It reacts instantly.

It drives your foot down on the gas pedal.

You are in motion before your conscious brain can form a full thought.

This is the hijack.

This is the biological default.

You desperately want to stop that trajectory.

You want to interrupt the yell.

You want to choose patience instead of panic.

But the switch is too fast.

The momentum is too great.

We need an emergency brake.

We need a self-control mechanism so simple, so instant, that it can override the biology of panic.

This is the art of the pause.

It is not silence.

It is not inaction.

It is a shift in internal attention.

It is the microscopic space between the trigger (the spilled juice) and your action (the verbal explosion).

This space is where freedom lives.

We are going to learn how to claim those three seconds.

Three seconds of intentional stillness.

Three seconds to move from programmed reaction to conscious choice.

Your regulation is not a luxury.

It is the tool.

It is the prerequisite for all wisdom that follows.

Ready to stop the rush?

The wisdom is waiting on the other side of the pause.

—★-★-★—

THE 3-SECOND PROTOCOL: HOW TO HIJACK YOUR BRAIN'S EMOTIONAL TRIGGER SYSTEM BEFORE THE CHAOS ERUPTS

YOU KNOW THE INSTANT. THAT FAMILIAR, TERRIFYING FLASH THAT happens when your child transitions from slightly annoying to full-blown meltdown territory.

It happens fast.

A child's defiance—a sudden push, a cruel word, a defiant glare—is a perfect biological trigger. Your own nervous system interprets it instantly as a threat to your safety, your authority, or your control.

In the fraction of a second, your emotional brain has already sent the signal: Fight!

Before you can even consciously form a rational thought, you are already moving. You are leaning in. Your voice is already pitched higher, sharper. You are about to become the parent you promised you wouldn't be.

We need a wedge. We need a circuit breaker.

This is the purpose of the 3-Second Protocol. It is a mandatory biological ceasefire. You do not respond to the child until you have completed this three-step sequence.

Your first response must always be self-regulation. Not response.

If you skip this, you are operating on primal instinct. If you use it, you operate from wisdom.

SECOND 1: PLANT YOUR FEET

The first physical response to activation is to feel loose, floating, and ready to flee or fight. You must counteract this immediately. Stop moving. Wherever you are, freeze. If you are standing, plant both feet firmly on the ground. Wiggle your toes inside your shoes. Feel the weight of your body anchoring down.

This simple physical act tells your nervous system, I am grounded. I am supported. I am not running. It interrupts the physical activation loop.

SECOND 2: THE FULL EXHALE

When we are stressed, our breath becomes short, shallow, and held high in the chest. This signals danger. You are going to override this signal immediately with one intentional, slow, complete exhale.

You don't need to take a big inhale first. Just push the air out. Hiss it out if you need to. Let your shoulders drop. Let your belly soften.

A slow exhale directly stimulates the Vagus nerve, which we discussed earlier. It is the fastest, simplest way to signal the safety center of your brain: The threat is minimal. I can relax. This is your brake pedal in action. Use it.

SECOND 3: NAME IT

After you have anchored your body and released the air, you have created a small amount of space. In this space, you perform one crucial cognitive task: You name the feeling you are currently experiencing.

Do this silently.

I feel intense frustration.

I feel disrespected.

I feel panic because I don't know what to do.

By naming the emotion, you engage the prefrontal cortex—the thinking, rational, wise part of your brain. You move the feeling from a boiling, amorphous reaction into a manageable, identifiable object. You are no longer being the anger; you are observing the anger.

Only once you have completed all three seconds—feet planted, breath released, feeling named—are you permitted to open your mouth and respond to your child.

Three seconds is all it takes to hijack the emotional trigger system. It is the shortest, most powerful investment you will ever make in your peace.

Practice it every single time the heat rises. It will become automatic. You will change your habit from reaction to intention.

—★-★-★—

THE SECRET WEAPON OF ELITE COMMUNICATORS: HOW SIMPLY NAMING YOUR ANGER DIFFUSES 80% OF ITS POWER

THE MOST PROFOUND COMMUNICATION SKILL YOU CAN MASTER ISN'T about the words you say to your child. It is about the words you say to yourself in the micro-moment before you open your mouth.

You know the feeling. The trigger happens. Maybe they break the third thing this morning. Maybe they scream at you in public. The heat rises. You feel the tightness in your chest. The surge of adrenaline. This is your nervous system preparing for battle. It is a primal, wordless panic.

If you react from that wordless, unnamed surge, you will yell. You will snap. You will withdraw. You will regret it instantly.

But what if you could install a linguistic dimmer switch in that critical moment?

This is where emotional literacy becomes your secret weapon. Before you address the child, you address the feeling. Silently. Internally. You label the state.

Do you feel anger? Often, what we call "anger" is a protective mask for something much more vulnerable. Anger is loud; fear is quiet. Anger is action; shame is frozen.

Ask yourself, "What is the truth of this feeling right now?"

The moment you can hold that hot, electric chaos and assign it a clear, concise label, you perform a cognitive miracle. You move the activity in your brain away from the volatile, reactive emotional center (the amygdala) and into the rational, executive control center (the prefrontal cortex).

Instead of thinking, "I am SO mad at this child," the internal dialogue shifts to: "I am feeling intense frustration that my boundaries were ignored." Or even better: "I feel deep disappointment right now." "I feel profound fear that I am failing as a parent."

Try this the next time the heat starts to rise. Just stop. Take that 3-second pause we talked about earlier, and name the feeling.

Why does naming it diffuse 80% of its power?

Because the emotional system's primary function is to get your attention and keep you safe. Once you have acknowledged the emotion—you have seen it, you have named it, you have understood its informational role—it no longer needs to scream. It drops its volume automatically.

What happens if you realize you are not actually angry, but terrified of what others will think of your parenting? Doesn't knowing that truth suddenly soften your gaze toward the child?

What if the rising feeling is not rage, but sheer, bone-deep exhaustion? When you label it "exhaustion," you realize that this is a need for rest, not a need for punishment. Your response shifts entirely.

Naming the emotion for yourself is not weakness; it is supreme strategic strength. Elite communicators do not suppress their feelings. They observe them. They categorize them. Then, and only then, do they decide which information is useful and which is just historical noise.

If you don't name it, it owns you. If you name it, you own it. Which parent do you want to be? The one driven by a nameless, historic surge, or the one calmly observing the data of the moment? Start practicing your internal diagnosis now. The clarity you find there will define the peace of your home.

THE 'EMERGENCY BRAKE' DRILL: 7 SENSORY HACKS TO IMMEDIATELY EXIT PANIC MODE (EVEN WHEN THEY ARE SCREAMING)

THE CHAOS IS PEAKING. THE SOUND IS A PHYSICAL THING NOW. IT hits your eardrums. It triggers that ancient alarm system in your brain. You feel the heat rising in your chest. That is the sympathetic nervous system taking control. The fight-or-flight response is ready to deploy.

We need to hit the brake.

We cannot reason ourselves out of this moment. Logic left the building five minutes ago. We must use a direct, physical shortcut to interrupt the alarm signal. We use sensory input. It forces your brain to acknowledge the reality of the present moment, rather than the perceived danger of the past or future.

This is the 'Emergency Brake' Drill. Deploy one or more of these instantly:

1. The Cold Wrist Dip. Find the nearest source of cold water. A bathroom sink. A water bottle. Run cold water over your wrists and the back of your neck for three seconds. This is biological shock. It instantly signals to your vagus nerve that the internal temperature needs adjusting, interrupting the panic signal.

2. The Texture Anchor. Reach out and touch something rough or cool. The grain of the wooden door. The cool metal of a doorknob. The harsh, uneven texture of the carpet. Fix your focus entirely on how that texture feels under your fingers.

3. The Heavy Foot. Press both feet firmly into the floor. Imagine you are trying to push the floor down into the basement. Feel the contact of

your heel. Feel the contact of your toes. This deep proprioceptive input grounds you into gravity and stability.

4. The Sour Interrupt. Keep a strong, sensory item nearby. A piece of gum. A tiny mint. A dropper of potent essential oil (peppermint, citrus) under your nose. The intense flavor or scent gives your brain a new, immediate problem to solve. It hijacks the focus from the screaming.

5. The Low Hum. When the child is yelling at high frequency, match it with low frequency. Place a hand on your stomach or chest and hum or groan deeply. Do not speak. The vibration created by humming activates the ventral vagal pathway, the calming branch of the nervous system.

6. The Color Spot. Look away from your child for three seconds. Scan the immediate room and locate three specific objects of the same color. A blue book, a blue stripe on a shirt, the blue light on the router. This forces the visual cortex to engage in a non-threatening task.

7. The Quick Squat. If you have the space, drop down quickly into a squat or a knee bend and stand back up. If you are seated, do a few rapid shoulder rolls. Small, vigorous muscle movements burn off the immediate adrenaline surge without requiring you to flee the scene.

These seven steps are not meant to solve the problem. They are only meant to solve your internal meltdown. Use them. Then, and only then, can you re-engage with your child from a regulated place. Your internal quiet is their greatest teacher.

—★-★-★—

HOW TO PERMANENTLY DELETE THE OLD TAPES THAT MAKE YOUR KIDS' DEFIANCE FEEL LIKE A PERSONAL ATTACK

That eye-roll hits differently. It cuts deep.

A simple act of defiance—a foot stomped, an arm crossed, a murmured "I hate you"—feels less like poor behavior and more like they looked into your soul and delivered a devastating verdict.

This is the oldest trigger in the book. Defiance. Disrespect. It is the instant activation button for parental rage or immediate emotional retreat.

Why?

Because it is almost never about the socks they won't put on.

It is about the Old Tapes.

Your nervous system is not reacting to a seven-year-old who is overwhelmed by bedtime. It is reacting to the ghost of a demanding parent, a critical boss, or a shaming partner from your past.

The child's behavior is the key that starts the recording. And the Old Tape begins to whisper its threats: You are losing control. You are weak. You are a failure. If you let them challenge you now, they will never respect you later.

We must stop these tapes cold. This requires decoupling the child's action from your historical emotional wound.

The process of deletion involves three crucial shifts in consciousness:

SHIFT ONE: NAME THE GHOST, NOT THE CHILD

When you feel that familiar spike of intense, disproportionate anger—the kind that makes your chest feel tight and your voice sound foreign—stop. Do not speak yet.

Ask yourself, "Who is this fury really for?"

Is it for the exhausted toddler in front of you? Or is it for the memory of yourself, shut down and dismissed as a child? Is the fear that your child will turn out spoiled, or is the fear that you will be seen as incompetent by outsiders?

Identify the specific narrative the Old Tape is playing: "I am being taken advantage of." "I am not good enough." "I am powerless."

Until you name the ghost of the past, you cannot effectively address the child in the present.

SHIFT TWO: REALITY CHECK THE THREAT LEVEL

Once you have identified the emotional wound, isolate it. Put a mental wall between that historical pain and the current situation.

Now, look at your child. Ask yourself: "Is this eight-year-old fundamentally threatening my safety or survival right now?"

The answer is almost always a resounding no.

They are testing a boundary. They are expressing a need clumsily. Their job, developmentally, is to test and stretch. They are not trying to destroy you; they are trying to figure out where the edge of the world is.

Disrespect is often distress. Defiance is often the only tool they have to communicate overwhelm.

By reality-checking the threat, you downgrade the situation from a five-alarm emergency (Old Tape volume) to a minor, manageable difficulty (Real Life volume).

SHIFT THREE: INSTALL THE NEW SOUNDTRACK

We replace the old, reactive storyline with a new, regulated, and conscious truth. This is your personal parental mantra during moments of high trigger.

When the anger flares and the Old Tape starts, actively recite your New Soundtrack.

Examples:

Old Tape: "They are defying me."

New Soundtrack: "This is a child practicing autonomy. Their resistance is not a measure of my worth."

Old Tape: "They are going to walk all over me."

New Soundtrack: "I am strong enough to hold this boundary gently. I do not need to yell to be powerful."

Old Tape: "I am a bad parent because they are acting this way."

New Soundtrack: "I am a safe parent, learning to respond, not react. Their behaviour is communication, not condemnation."

This shift is not a one-time event; it is a moment-to-moment choice. Every time you consciously choose the New Soundtrack over the Old Tape, you weaken the historical connection. You starve the ghost of its power.

You are training your nervous system to understand: The past threat is over. The child in front of me is safe. And I am safe, too. The defiance may continue, but the feeling of personal attack will diminish, replaced by quiet, steady authority.

CHAPTER FOUR

—★-★-★—

SPEAKING PEACE: THE QUIET COMMUNICATION STYLE THAT STOPS POWER STRUGGLES BEFORE THEY START (AND WHAT NEVER TO SAY)

We have built the anchor. We have found the pause. Now, we must speak from that grounded place.

The biggest mistake regulated parents make is applying old, dysregulated communication scripts while their body is calm. They press the internal brake pedal, then immediately launch into a twenty-minute lecture designed to inflict shame or control.

This defeats the entire purpose.

Communication is not about the words you use. It is about the frequency you broadcast. When your nervous system is steady, your voice drops. Your pace slows. Your body language softens. This quiet transmission—the speaking peace—is the critical element that stops power struggles before they can even gain traction.

When a child is escalated, their neocortex (the thinking, planning part of the brain) is offline. They are operating from the ancient, reactive parts of the brain. They cannot process logic. They cannot grasp future consequences. They can only detect one thing: safety or threat.

If you match their volume, match their frustration, or try to logic them out of their feelings, you are broadcasting a threat. You are essentially saying, "The person who is supposed to keep me safe is now losing control." This instantly intensifies their defense state, guaranteeing defiance.

Speaking peace means adjusting your output to maximize their reception of safety.

The single most powerful communication technique available to you is the regulation of your own vocal tone. A low, slow, melodic voice is the sound of safety. It tells the child's vagus nerve: I hear you. I see your upset. But I am not upset. I have this.

Refuse to match their intensity. If they yell, whisper. If they race, slow down. When you do this, you are not manipulating them; you are lending them your calm. You are regulating the environment so their system has a chance to settle.

What NEVER to Say

If there is one category of language that sabotages connection immediately, it is language that forces them to defend their feelings or their logic. Avoid these two common pitfalls, especially during moments of escalation:

1. Anything that begins with "Why...": "Why did you hit your sister?" "Why can't you just listen?" Why questions are intellectual demands at an emotional moment. They feel like an interrogation. The child does not know the "why." They only know the feeling that drove the action. Asking them to justify a defensive reaction only compounds their shame and frustration.

2. Any phrase that minimizes the distress: "It's not a big deal." "Stop crying over nothing." "You're fine." Minimizing their reality communicates profound disconnection. It teaches them that their internal experience is wrong or inconvenient. This is the surest route to rebellion and emotional suppression.

Instead, start with acknowledgment and acceptance. Focus on connection before you ever attempt correction. This is the difference between a compliant child and a connected, cooperating child.

Correction without connection guarantees resistance.

The child needs to feel seen and heard before they can accept a boundary or a consequence. Think of connection as the required lubricant for compliance. You must fill their emotional cup before you can ask them to do hard things, like stop an activity they love or accept a disappointment.

This requires a radical shift in pacing.

When your child is distressed, the protocol is simple:

1. The Pause (Chapter 3 work).

2. Physical Proximity (Move closer, drop low).

3. Name the Feeling, Not the Behavior: "Wow, that is so frustrating when the block tower falls." "You seem really angry right now." "You are disappointed that we have to leave the park."

Notice we are validating the feeling first. We are not validating the behavior. We are simply saying: Your inner world makes sense, even if your outer actions need limits.

Once the feeling is named and accepted, a small window of opportunity opens. Only then can you set the boundary or guide the behavior: "You are angry the tower fell. And the rule is we use gentle hands. Can you stomp your feet instead of throwing the blocks?"

This style of communication separates the child from the problem. The child is good; the behavior is the signal of distress.

The ultimate power in peaceful communication comes when we, the adults, get honest about our own inner state without outsourcing the responsibility for that state to the child.

We use "I feel" statements not as a passive-aggressive tool to manipulate behavior, but as a pure statement of our internal reality, which then informs the limit we must set. The Precision Formula looks like this:

I feel [specific emotion, not a judgment] when [non-blaming observation of the situation] because [my specific, primary need is not being met]. Therefore, [this is the clear boundary I am setting].

Example of failure: "I feel like you are being a bad listener when you ignore me, and you need to stop doing that right now." (Blames, uses judgment.)

Example of Speaking Peace: "I feel stressed and rushed when I see you still playing with your shoes five minutes after I asked you to put them on, because I need to feel like we can leave the house on time. I am going to hold the shoes for you now, and we will try again tomorrow."

This formula keeps the focus on your adult capacity and your needs. It is clear. It is empathetic to your own limits. And most importantly, it offers a boundary without instilling a drop of guilt in the child. The boundary is an act of self-care, not an act of punishment.

This approach requires us to be humble. We are human, and we are not perfect. We will be dysregulated. We will yell. We will snap. We will say the wrong thing.

The post-meltdown protocol—repair—is often more critical to the child's long-term emotional intelligence than the original mistake was. When you model healthy repair, you teach your child the most priceless lesson of all: how to recover from emotional failure.

If you yell, your only task is to return to regulation, and then return to the child. Find them. Drop your voice low. Make eye contact.

"Hey, I want to come back to what happened a few minutes ago. I yelled when I spoke to you, and I am sorry. That was too loud and too fast. I got frustrated when I saw the mess, and I let my feelings take over. That wasn't your fault. I am working on keeping my voice calm. Can we have a hug?"

When you admit you messed up, you are not weakening your authority. You are strengthening your connection. You are teaching them that it is possible to make a mistake, own it, repair the relationship, and move forward. You are installing the most sophisticated regulation tool in their arsenal: resilience.

This is the cycle of peace: Self-regulation leads to peaceful speech, which allows for connection, which reinforces the child's sense of safety, which allows them to accept limits, which ultimately brings regulation to the entire home.

—★-★-★—

THE COUNTER-INTUITIVE POWER OF BEING COMPLETELY SILENT WHEN YOUR CHILD NEEDS YOU MOST

YOUR CHILD STARTS TALKING. MAYBE COMPLAINING. MAYBE CRYING. Maybe just unloading the pressure of a difficult school day.

Immediately, the parent urge kicks in.

Fix it. Problem-solve it. Rush to judgment. We think that caring means acting. We believe that love means having the perfect answer. This is our nervous system seeking control. It wants to quiet the distress—theirs, and the distress the sound causes in us.

I want you to try the opposite.

When your child starts to share a problem, stop moving.

Stop washing the dishes. Stop scrolling your phone. Turn off the podcast playing in the background.

Drop your shoulders. Let the tension drain from your neck.

Do not look away. But most importantly: Say nothing.

This is radical stillness.

We are so practiced at filling every space with noise. With input. With advice. Silence feels like a failure of parenting. It feels awkward. It feels like you are withholding.

But in reality, silence is the greatest gift of presence.

Your child is not looking for advice at that very moment. They are looking for an echo. They are looking for a mirror. They want proof that their overwhelming inner experience is real and valid.

When you interrupt their story—even with the most gentle, perfect solution—the message their nervous system receives is: Stop feeling that way. Your feelings make the adult uncomfortable.

The feeling immediately goes into hiding. The story shuts down. The connection is severed.

True listening is a physical act.

It is not about waiting for your turn to talk. It is about becoming a completely safe container.

Adopt an open posture. Turn your whole body toward them. Hands relaxed. Sit if they are sitting. Get down to their eye level if they are standing.

Look at their face, maybe their hands. And breathe. Slow, steady breaths.

Let their words fill the entire space between you. Allow the intensity of their feeling to exist without trying to neutralize it or fix it. Let the silence hang there, rich and full.

You are communicating safety, not through words, but through your anchored presence. You are literally lending them your calm nervous system.

Do not move until they have completed their thought. Do not nod furiously. Do not even make too many reflective sounds. Just stillness.

Wait for the pause. Wait until they truly stop talking and look at you. That silence is the sign that the feeling has been witnessed. The story is complete. The tension has dissipated.

Only then, perhaps, can you gently ask: "Do you want me to listen more, or do you want help solving this?"

But often, by the time they finish talking, the worst of the crisis is already over. They don't need a fix.

They needed to be heard.

Silence is the deepest form of respect.

—★-★-★—

WARNING: WHY CORRECTING BEHAVIOUR BEFORE YOU CONNECT WITH THE FEELING GUARANTEES A REBELLIOUS TEENAGER

We are wired for efficiency. We see a problem. We want to solve it.

Your child is screaming because they don't want to put on their shoes. You see the behavior: defiance. You jump immediately to correction. "Stop yelling. Get your shoes on right now or we will be late! This is unacceptable."

This is where the entire learning process crashes.

Your child is not thinking logically in that moment. They are not plotting rebellion. They are flooded. They are operating from their emotional, defensive state.

When you approach a nervous system in distress with pure logic or consequence, what do they hear?

They hear: Your feelings are wrong. Your pain is inconvenient. Your reaction is a problem I need to shut down.

This message is toxic to connection. It teaches them to compartmentalize their distress. It teaches them to hide their inner world from you.

Correction before connection is a physiological mistake.

The goal is to get the child's brain out of the defensive Red Zone and back into the regulated Green Zone. The only way back to Green is through the feeling of safety. Validation is the safety switch.

Connection must always precede correction.

Validation is not agreement. You do not have to agree that their refusal to wear shoes is rational. You just have to recognize the feeling beneath the refusal.

Validation is recognizing the internal story.

"You are so angry right now. You wanted to choose your shoes and that made you mad when I helped you. I hear how frustrated you are." (Connection)

Now, and only now, is the door open. Now the logical brain can receive input.

"I know you are furious. That frustration is real. And the rule is, we must wear our shoes to school. You can be frustrated and still put them on." (Correction and Safety).

When you skip that crucial validation step, you force the child to defend their legitimate emotion. They have to fight for the right to feel angry, or sad, or afraid. They must prove their feeling is real.

When a child constantly has to fight for their feelings to be acknowledged, they build a protective wall. That wall becomes the rebellious teenager. The one who won't talk. The one who shuts the door in your face.

They are simply protecting their inner landscape from judgment. They have been conditioned to believe that sharing their distress leads only to consequences, not empathy.

You want a teenager who talks to you about their struggles? You must lay the groundwork today. You must make it safe to be messy. You must validate the feeling even when you cannot tolerate the behaviour.

Validation disarms the defence. It creates trust. It is the sound of the brain switching back on. Only then can the lesson land.

THE PRECISION FORMULA FOR 'I FEEL' STATEMENTS THAT GETS YOUR NEEDS MET WITHOUT INSTILLING GUILT

We often confuse stating our feelings with expressing blame. Most "I feel" statements fall flat because they are thinly veiled accusations.

"I feel angry when you don't listen to me."

That sentence, while seemingly healthy, lands on your child like a punch. Why? Because the child hears: "You are responsible for my anger. If you acted differently, I wouldn't be upset." This instantly triggers their defensive nervous system. They stop listening and start defending themselves or, worse, internalizing guilt.

The Precision Formula removes the blame by focusing only on observable actions and the adult's internal need for safety and structure. It is a three-part structure designed to be emotionally honest, but physiologically non-threatening.

The Formula is:

1. State the observable, neutral situation.
2. State your internal feeling, owned entirely by you.
3. State the action or boundary needed for your regulation.

Let's look at how this works in practice.

If your child throws their jacket on the kitchen floor for the fifth time, your immediate internal reaction is probably anger and exhaustion.

The Blaming Statement (Instilling Guilt):

"I feel furious when you treat our home like a trash heap. Why can't you ever remember?"

(Emotional impact: Shame and resentment. Focus is on the child's character failure.)

The Precision Statement (Getting Needs Met):

"When I see the jacket left on the floor near the kitchen, I feel highly frustrated and disorganized. My brain needs our shared space to be tidy so I can relax and prepare dinner. I need you to please pick up the jacket now and hang it up."

(Emotional impact: Clarity and cooperation. Focus is on the parent's internal state and a request for mutual regulatory space.)

Notice the power shift. You are not saying the child made you feel frustrated. You are simply reporting that in the presence of that situation, that is how your system responds. This teaches your child that your emotions are valuable data, but they are not the child's responsibility to fix permanently.

When you use this precise language, you are modeling three things that are infinitely valuable for your child's future:

1. Emotional Honesty: You are accurately labeling your internal state, moving beyond generic anger.

2. Boundary Clarity: You are clearly defining what is acceptable for your own safety and function.

3. Personal Agency: You are teaching them that when they feel an emotion, they can identify the underlying need and ask for it directly, rather than resorting to passive aggression or demands.

The secret power of this formula lies in the final step: stating the action needed for your regulation. You are not asking them to stop doing something—you are asking them to start doing something that supports the family unit and, critically, supports your ability to be a calm parent. This is cooperation rooted in empathy, not compliance rooted in fear.

This approach transforms the interaction from a personal attack on their behavior into a negotiation based on mutual respect and shared space.

You teach them that boundaries are not punishments; boundaries are the way that safe people love one another.

—★-★-★—

THE SECRET POST-MELTDOWN PROTOCOL: HOW ADMITTING YOU MESSED UP INSTALLS REGULATION TOOLS IN YOUR CHILD (PRICELESS LESSON)

YOU SNAPPED.

It was louder than you meant it to be. The tone was sharper. The frustration boiled over and you said something you instantly regretted.

Welcome to being human.

The common myth in parenting is that good parents never lose their temper. This is impossible. We are wired to react when we are exhausted, overwhelmed, or triggered. The rupture, the moment of dysregulation, is inevitable.

The magic—the priceless lesson you can only teach through failure—is the repair.

When you lose control, your child's nervous system goes on high alert. They need to know that the safe person (you) can become unsafe for a moment, but that the safety of the relationship is always restored.

Repair is the single most important lesson in emotional regulation you will ever teach.

When you go back to them after the dust settles, you are teaching them how to install their own internal regulation tools. You are modeling self-correction.

The Secret Post-Meltdown Protocol is simple, quick, and non-negotiable.

STEP 1: OWN THE SNAP

Find them when you are calm. Get low. Look them in the eyes and start with your accountability. "I am sorry I yelled." Do not add a 'but.' Do not say, "I'm sorry I yelled, but you wouldn't listen." That invalidates the apology and shifts the blame. Own your side of the street, completely.

STEP 2: NAME YOUR INTERNAL STATE

Explain briefly what happened inside you. "I was feeling overwhelmed by the noise, and my brain went into a panic reaction." Or, "I was very frustrated because I felt unheard." This is crucial. You teach them that feelings are information, not a script for bad behavior.

STEP 3: APOLOGIZE FOR THE IMPACT

Acknowledge how your action affected them. "When I yelled, I made you feel scared. That was not okay." You are validating their experience of the event.

STEP 4: REAFFIRM SAFETY AND RECONNECT

Confirm that the relationship is safe, even after the storm. "I always love you, and my job is to keep you safe. My frustration is my problem, and I am working on staying calm." Then, offer physical reconnection: a hug, a quiet moment, or just sitting together.

This process is not just about making the child feel better. It is about actively strengthening the child's vagal tone. You show them that big feelings don't break the world. You model the pathway back to calm, stability, and connection.

Every time you initiate a genuine repair, you are effectively installing the 'reset button' in their own operating system. You are teaching them: Conflict is survivable. Rupture leads to repair. And self-correction is the greatest form of strength.

Your biggest failure becomes your most profound teaching moment. Never skip the repair. It is the curriculum for resilience.

CHAPTER FIVE

—★-★-★—

DECODING THEIR DISTRESS: WHY THEIR WORST BEHAVIOR IS A SECRET MESSAGE (AND HOW TO INSTANTLY TRANSLATE IT)

You have reached the pivotal point of this work. This is where we stop treating the symptom and start healing the source.

For years, we have been conditioned to view challenging behavior—tantrums, defiance, lashing out, withdrawal—as intentional acts of malice or poor discipline. We call it "misbehavior." We assume the child is choosing to make our lives difficult.

This assumption is not just exhausting; it is fundamentally flawed. It sets us up for continuous conflict because it misidentifies the messenger.

Your child is not giving you a hard time. They are having a hard time.

Their worst, most explosive, and most infuriating actions are not failures of character. They are sophisticated, high-volume distress signals broadcast directly from their nervous system. They are the physiological evidence that their internal resources have run out.

A child does not choose dysregulation. A nervous system simply responds to what it perceives as danger, threat, or overwhelming demand.

When you look at a child mid-meltdown, you are not looking at a spoiled tyrant demanding control. You are looking at a small human experiencing a complete system overload. The prefrontal cortex—the part responsible for logic, reason, and impulse control—has been temporarily taken offline by the survival mechanisms deep within the brainstem.

Think of the child's body as a complex machine that is short-circuiting. If you were driving a car and the warning lights flashed, you wouldn't kick the dashboard. You would pull over and examine the engine.

Our job as the regulated adult is to stop kicking the dashboard. Our job is to translate the noise.

When a child hits, the message is not, "I hate you." The message is, "I am carrying an intolerable amount of energy and I do not have the capacity to regulate it safely."

When a child shuts down and refuses to speak, the message is not, "I am disrespecting you." The message is, "My system is in freeze mode; the threat is too overwhelming, and I need to disappear to feel safe."

This chapter provides the tools to instantly decode these signals. By applying the nervous system lens, we remove the personal offense from the equation. We move from seeing an attack to seeing a plea.

Once you master this shift, everything changes. The chaos stops feeling like a personal failure and starts feeling like solvable, biological data. You stop reacting automatically with frustration and start responding intentionally with connection, becoming the safe harbor your child's distressed system is frantically searching for.

—★-★-★—

EXPOSED: WHY PUNISHING A TANTRUM IS LIKE TREATING A FEVER WITH A HAMMER (AND THE BETTER WAY TO SOOTHE THE SOURCE)

A TANTRUM IS NOT DEFIANCE. IT IS DISTRESS.

We have been taught for generations to view a child's meltdown as a behavior problem. We see it as intentional disobedience. We see it as manipulation. This faulty belief system is what leads us to apply punishments—time-outs, forced compliance, shaming language.

But this is like standing over a child with a searing high fever and yelling at the thermometer. You are attacking the symptom. You are attacking the measurement. You are missing the root cause entirely.

The root cause is always a dysregulated nervous system.

When a child's frustration threshold is breached—due to hunger, fatigue, overstimulation, or fear—their executive functioning brain goes dark. The logic center closes for business. What takes over is the core survival system, the primitive brain.

The tantrum is the visible manifestation of that system desperately trying to discharge overwhelm.

When they are screaming, they are in the biological state of Fight. Their body is releasing hormones designed to confront a threat.

When they are throwing themselves on the floor and refusing to move, they may be in Freeze. Their system is overwhelmed and shutting down, waiting for safety.

When they lash out or hit a sibling, they are in pure, unadulterated defense. This is not disrespect. This is survival.

If we respond to this physiological state with punishment, we compound the stress. We confirm for their body that the environment is, indeed, hostile. We tell them: "I cannot handle your pain. You are unsafe when you feel big emotions."

Punishing a survival mechanism is senseless. It is cruel. It is useless. It teaches the child nothing about regulation. It only teaches them to fear their own internal experience and hide their distress next time.

You cannot logically reason with a child whose logic center is offline. You cannot impose compliance on a nervous system that is fighting for its life.

The better way is to move past the behavior and immediately search for the source. What is the infection causing the fever? What is the trigger causing the system overload?

Are they tired? Are they hungry? Do they feel unheard? Have they had too much sensory input?

The moment we translate the behavior into a feeling—I see you are angry (the behavior), but I know you feel scared and overwhelmed (the feeling)—we change everything. We are no longer addressing the external chaos. We are soothing the internal source.

We do not use a hammer on the fever. We use connection, calm presence, and co-regulation to treat the pain. We regulate their state, and the behavior automatically softens. This is the difference between temporary forced compliance and lasting emotional regulation.

—★-★-★—

THE PARENT'S 3-COLOR ZONE CHECK: A SIMPLE 10-SECOND TOOL FOR KNOWING EXACTLY WHAT YOUR CHILD NEEDS RIGHT NOW

You need speed when parenting. You do not have time for a complex behavioral analysis when your child is screaming in the grocery aisle.

You need a 10-second tool.

The Parent's 3-Color Zone Check is a simple physiological assessment. It instantly tells you what part of your child's brain is running the show—and therefore, what they desperately need from you right now.

Forget malicious intent. Forget discipline for a moment. Just assess the nervous system.

GREEN ZONE: REGULATED AND READY

The State: This is the resting state. The prefrontal cortex is online. The Vagus nerve is functioning smoothly. Your child feels safe, connected, and available.

How It Looks: Curiosity. Flexibility. Using their words clearly. Laughing. Accepting reasonable limits. Good eye contact. They are operating from their most authentic, intelligent self.

What They Need: Connection, time, and teaching.

This is the only time boundaries, rules, and coping skills can be successfully taught and internalized. Use this time to build the foundation. Your job is to stay regulated and enjoy the stability.

YELLOW ZONE: ACTIVATED AND ALERT

The State: This is the warning light. The sympathetic nervous system is activating. They are feeling a rush of stress hormones. They are preparing for minor fight or flight. They are moving toward dysregulation.

How It Looks: Whining. Increased volume. Fidgeting. Excessive silliness. Boundary testing. Quick frustration over minor things (the crusts are wrong, the toy broke). Agitation or sudden inability to focus.

What They Need: Co-regulation and prevention.

This is the moment to intervene with stillness, not conversation. Pause the activity. Use a low, slow tone of voice. Offer predictable transition cues. Provide physical co-regulation—a hug, a hand on the back, a sip of water. Your goal is to gently guide them back to Green before Red takes over.

RED ZONE: DEFENSIVE AND SHUTDOWN

THE STATE: TOTAL SYSTEM OVERLOAD. FIGHT, FLIGHT, OR FREEZE IS fully engaged. The thinking brain is offline. They are operating purely from a survival mechanism. This is not defiance; it is defense.

How It Looks: Full, non-negotiable meltdown. Hitting, kicking, or running away (fight/flight). Complete emotional shutdown, staring blankly, going silent, hiding (freeze). Inability to hear or process verbal instruction.

What They Need: Safety, space, and a steady presence.

STOP everything. Do not talk. Do not teach. Do not rationalize. Move slowly. Maintain proximity if it is safe for both of you. You are a biological shock absorber. Focus only on your own regulation. Breathe deeply and lend your calm. The brain cannot learn in Red. Your only job is to provide safe harbor until their system cycles back down to Yellow or Green.

The entire assessment takes seconds. Is their body flexible or rigid? Are their eyes open and curious, or tight and darting? Can they hear you? Once you identify the zone, you instantly know your mission. You shift from confused reactor to intentional regulator.

—★–★–★—

THE UNSPOKEN TRANSFER: HOW YOUR REGULATED PRESENCE ACTS AS A BIOLOGICAL SHOCK ABSORBER FOR THEIR PANIC

IMAGINE YOUR CHILD IS A SHIP CAUGHT IN A STORM. THEY ARE pitching and rolling, waves of emotion crashing over the deck. You, the parent, are not just the captain; you are the lighthouse. You are the immovable structure they can orient themselves toward.

This is the principle of co-regulation. It is the most powerful tool you possess, far more potent than any time-out or reward chart. Your presence acts as a biological shock absorber for their panic.

When a child is dysregulated—screaming, hitting, or frozen—their nervous system is in a high-alert defensive state. They are sending out distress signals. Their brain is literally scanning the environment, searching for a sign that the danger is not catastrophic.

The most important sign they scan for is you.

When you meet their chaos with chaos—yelling, anxiety, or withdrawal—you confirm the threat. Their system screams, "The lighthouse is burning down! We are truly doomed!"

But when you intentionally regulate yourself first (Chapter 2 and 3 work), you offer a different, stronger signal. You lend your regulated system to theirs. Your internal state becomes their temporary safe harbor. Their body recognizes, on a deep, physiological level, that if the largest, most crucial person in the environment is calm, then the current situation is survivable.

This transfer of calm is not magical thinking; it is the fundamental mechanism of human connection. We are wired to stabilize each other.

How do you physically implement this unspoken transfer?

1. PROXIMITY OVER DISTANCE

When a child is overwhelmed, do not send them away to "calm down" unless they specifically request space. Instead, decrease the physical distance between you. You don't need to force a hug or invade their space. Simply sit or stand closer. Your steady, regulated body becomes a physical boundary against their rising anxiety. A child leaning against a parent, even minimally, is leveraging the parent's ventral vagal system to quiet their own.

2. THE POWER OF STEADY TOUCH

If your child is open to touch, use deep, slow, steady contact. Avoid frantic rubbing or quick pats, which can feel activating or impatient. Place a warm, firm hand on their back, their shoulder, or their thigh. The purpose of this touch is to communicate safety through pressure. Slow, sustained pressure helps organize the nervous system, signalling to the brain that the body is grounded. This is why weighted blankets work; you are essentially providing a focused, weighted presence.

3. THE LOW, SLOW VOCAL TONE

The human voice is a highly tuned regulatory instrument. When you are panicked, your voice goes high-pitched and quick—the acoustic signal of alarm. When you are regulated, your voice naturally drops in pitch and slows in tempo. This low, modulated tone is decoded by the child's middle ear as a safety cue. Speak slowly. Speak quietly. Use a slightly sing-song cadence if you can manage it. Say only what is essential: "I see you are upset. I am right here." This non-verbal communication is 80% of the co-regulation process.

By slowing your movements, lowering your voice, and offering steady proximity, you become a living, breathing biological cue of safety. You are communicating, without using words, the single most important message a distressed child can receive: You are safe, and I can handle this.

SETTING LIMITS THAT STICK: THE COMPASSIONATE BOUNDARY FORMULA THAT BUILDS SELF-CONTROL INSTEAD OF RESENTMENT

WE OFTEN THINK OF BOUNDARIES AS A WALL WE BUILD AGAINST THE child. That is the wrong image. A boundary is a fence. It is a container. It provides safe, predictable structure so the child's nervous system can relax.

A shaky boundary creates anxiety. A firm boundary delivered with calm creates safety.

The greatest sabotage to a boundary is delivering it while you are dysregulated. If you yell the limit, the child hears the threat, not the rule. They go into fight/flight. They resist the limit because they are fighting your fear.

Your first step is always the pause. Regulate yourself. Speak from your steady core.

The Compassionate Boundary Formula works every time. It has three rapid parts.

The first part is connection: Validate the feeling.

Before you address the behaviour, acknowledge the internal state. This is critical. Misbehaviour is a message. We must read the message before we deliver the reply.

You look so angry that screen time is over. I see how much you wanted to keep playing that game. I understand you are frustrated that I said no.

Validation is not agreement. You are not agreeing that the rule should change. You are agreeing that the emotion is real. This step disarms the defence mechanism instantly. It communicates: I see your heart.

The second part is correction: State the limit clearly.

Use as few words as possible. Do not lecture. Do not shame. Focus on the behaviour or the rule, not the child's character.

Validation: I know you are angry about the schedule change.

Limit: But hitting your sister is not okay. My job is to keep everyone safe.

Validation: I know you are disappointed you can't have that toy.

Limit: We are not buying that today. That is my decision.

The boundary is firm. It is short. It must be delivered without wavering, but always with warmth. This builds inner self-control because the child trusts the consistency.

The third part is co-regulation: Reassure safety.

After the limit is set, the child may still protest. They may cry or escalate. This is where you lend your calm. You do not isolate them. You provide co-regulation.

You can be mad about the limit, and I will sit here with you while you are mad. Your feelings are welcome, but the hitting stops now. Let's breathe together.

The power of this formula lies in its duality. You accept the emotion fully. You do not accept the dangerous or destructive behaviour. The child learns: My parent loves me even when I feel enormous disappointment. My parent is strong enough to hold the line. This is the definition of safety.

Boundaries that stick are boundaries delivered from a regulated nervous system. They are limits that reassure: I am the safe adult, and I have the steady frame.

CHAPTER SIX

—★-★-★—

THE RESILIENT CHILD: HOW TO IMMUNIZE YOUR KIDS AGAINST ANXIETY SO THEY THRIVE WHEN YOU'RE NOT AROUND

For five chapters, we worked together. We stabilized the adult. We decoded the message hidden in the chaos. We learned to lend our calm.

Lending your calm—that's called co-regulation. It is essential. It is the foundation of trust.

But what happens when you're not there? When they are taking a test? When they are facing a mean kid on the playground? When the future feels too big to hold?

We don't want our children to be dependent on our presence to feel safe. We want them to internalize the toolkit. We want them to carry the same unshakable security you have built within yourself. This is the ultimate gift of nervous system work: true, deep, independent resilience.

Resilience is not the absence of struggle. It is the ability to return to baseline after the struggle hits. It's the ability to pause and regulate when the world is demanding a reaction. This chapter is about teaching them how to build that return path.

The shift is profound. We move from asking, “How do I fix this feeling for them?” to “How do I help them observe and manage this feeling themselves?”

This is not about giving them a breathing exercise they hate. This is about inviting them into the process of understanding their own marvelous, complicated wiring. We are teaching them to become the safe house for their own emotions. That’s the true immunization against lifelong anxiety.

—★-★-★—

BEYOND THE BREATHING BALL: A STEP-BY-STEP GUIDE TO HELPING YOUR CHILD DESIGN THEIR OWN ANXIETY-PROOF TOOLKIT

THE "BREATHING BALL" IS A WONDERFUL STARTING POINT. IT OFFERS a tangible visualization for breath. But let’s be honest: when the stress response is screaming at full volume—when the child is in full physiological distress—a simple visualization often fails.

The reason is simple: regulation is deeply personal. What calms one child (a quiet dark room) will trigger the sensory system of another (a feeling of isolation). Your child needs tools that are custom-built for their unique nervous system fingerprint.

This process is not about assigning coping skills. It is about becoming a curious detective alongside your child, helping them discover which levers and buttons inside their body truly activate the calm response. This shifts their mindset from dependency ("I need Mom to fix me") to self-efficacy ("I know how to regulate myself").

The following steps guide you in co-creating a genuinely anxiety-proof, personalized toolkit.

STEP ONE: THE REGULATION INVENTORY (WHAT ARE THEY ALREADY DOING?)

Before you introduce anything new, take inventory of their natural, often subconscious, attempts at regulation. Your child is already trying to cope; we just need to validate and refine those attempts.

The Clues: When your child is slightly stressed (yellow zone), what small, repetitive actions do they perform?

Do they chew on their collar, suck on their thumb, or bite their nails? (Oral/Vocal seeking)

Do they jiggle their leg, tap their pencil, or constantly shift in their chair? (Movement/Proprioceptive seeking)

Do they seek out specific textures, pull their hood over their eyes, or hum softly? (Sensory modulation)

The Conversation: Instead of correcting the behaviour ("Stop chewing your sleeve"), name the function ("It looks like your mouth needs some input right now to feel steady"). Explain that these actions are their body's smart way of trying to feel safe.

STEP TWO: THE SENSORY EXPERIMENT (THE LOW-STAKES TRYOUT)

You cannot introduce a new coping skill during a crisis. The brain simply won't access it. This step requires dedicated, quiet time to experiment. The goal is to see how different sensory inputs impact their physical body, then let the child choose their favourites.

Movement and Proprioception (Deep Pressure): Experiment with activities that provide heavy feedback to the joints and muscles, which is incredibly grounding.

Push-and-Pull: Have them push their hands hard against a wall for five seconds. Does that help the jitters?

Weighted Pressure: Try a heavy blanket or a tight squeeze hug. Does the weight feel comforting or restrictive?

Jumping: Ten hard jumps in place. Does the impact help shake out the energy?

Oral and Vocal Input: The jaw is highly linked to the vagus nerve. Rhythmic chewing or making sound is a quick regulator.

Chewing Tools: Offer crunch foods (carrots, pretzel rods) or non-toxic chewelry.

Humming and Singing: Hum a long, low tone. Does the vibration feel stabilizing in their chest?

Touch and Temperature: Explore immediate, powerful sensory shifts.

Cold: Holding an ice cube or running wrists under cold water.

Texture: Keep a soft piece of velvet, a smooth stone, or a bristly brush nearby. Which texture makes their shoulders drop?

STEP THREE: THE ASSEMBLY AND NAMING (CREATING OWNERSHIP)

Once you have identified three to five tools that reliably shift their physical state, formalize the toolkit. Let the child take the lead in how this is organized.

The Box: Get a small box or bag they decorate themselves. This is not the parent's box; it is the child's.

The Names: Help them name the tools based on function. Instead of "Breathing," it might be "The Balloon Belly" or "Smelling the Soup." Instead of "Pushing the wall," it might be "The Power Push."

The Map: For younger children, create a simple visual map showing the tool and where it helps their body (e.g., drawing a picture of chewing gum next to a picture of a calm face).

The Key Rule: Every tool must be something they can access instantly and independently. If they need you to hand it to them, it's a co-regulation tool, not a self-regulation tool.

Step Four: The Practice Run (Implementing When Calm)

The final step is practicing deployment. Do not wait for the inevitable moment of high stress.

Simulation: Play-act small moments of frustration. "Oh no, my tower fell down! I feel frustrated! What tool should I try?"

The Gentle Prompt: When you see their early signs of activation (fidgeting, furrowed brow), use gentle curiosity: "I notice your foot is tapping fast. Does your body need a tool from your box right now?"

Celebrate Success: When they proactively use a tool, acknowledge the skill, not just the outcome. "I noticed you took five big sips of water before asking me that question. That was such smart self-management. How does your body feel now?"

By giving your child this agency, you are teaching them the greatest lesson in resilience: that they are not victims of their emotions, but the skilled architects of their own internal calm.

STOP SUPPRESSING, START ACCEPTING: THE COUNTER-INTUITIVE LESSON THAT TURNS INTENSE EMOTIONS INTO SOURCES OF STRENGTH

The primal urge of every parent is to stop their child's distress. We hate the sound of genuine sorrow. We cannot tolerate the volcanic heat of their anger. So what do we do? We become rapid-fire suppressors.

Stop crying. Calm down. Don't be sad about that. It's just a toy.

We have good intentions. We want to protect them from pain. We want quiet. But suppression is the greatest saboteur of emotional strength. When we teach a child to stuff their anger or hide their fear, we teach them that their internal experience is dangerous. We teach them that parts of themselves are unwelcome.

But feelings are facts. They are pure biological information. They are the data points flashing on the dashboard of their nervous system.

When you suppress anger, it doesn't disappear. It turns inward. It becomes anxiety. It becomes physical tension. It becomes rigid control. Or it explodes, eventually, because the internal pressure gauge maxed out.

The counter-intuitive lesson is this: We must teach our children to lean into the discomfort. We must teach them emotional tolerance.

Tolerance means accepting the existence of the feeling without demanding it change immediately. It means creating space for the intensity.

Your role as the regulated parent is to lend your calm nervous system as a container for their storm.

You say: I see you are furious. It is okay to be furious. Fury is a big, powerful feeling.

Notice the difference. You are not saying: Stop feeling furious. You are not saying: Your furious feeling is bad.

You are validating the data point. You are accepting the information.

Feelings are information, not directives.

This is the distinction that creates resilient human beings.

The feeling of anger is information that a boundary has been violated or a need has gone unmet. That anger does not command the child to hit the wall or scream at the sibling. It is simply a signal.

The feeling of anxiety is information that the system has detected a potential threat. That anxiety does not command the child to flee the room or refuse the task. It is simply a warning.

When you help your child identify and accept the feeling—My chest is tight. My hands feel hot. I am feeling grief right now—you teach them to observe it, rather than become enslaved by it. You are helping them develop the emotional muscle to sit with difficulty.

This spacious acceptance is the source of inner strength.

It is how intense emotions transform from disruptive forces into manageable energy. We want children who can feel big things and still remain whole. We want children who trust their feelings but know they have a choice about what to do next.

Your permission for them to feel big emotions is the ultimate gift of safety. You are proving, moment by moment, that the strong currents of life will not destroy them, because you are there, holding the space, steady and true.

THE PHYSICAL FIX: 7 SENSORY ACTIVITIES THAT INSTANTLY RESET A FRIZZED-OUT NERVOUS SYSTEM (WORKS IN 90 SECONDS)

THE FASTEST ROUTE TO A CALM BRAIN IS ALWAYS THROUGH THE physical body.

When a child (or an adult) is in a high-alert state, the prefrontal cortex —the part that handles logic and reasoning—is offline. You cannot reason with a panic response. You must intervene physiologically.

This is the power of sensory awareness. We use intentional, physical input to send a clear message to the nervous system: "You are safe now." Sensory input is the raw data that overrides the alarm bell. It works immediately. It requires zero conscious thought.

Here are seven sensory activities designed to instantly interrupt sympathetic (fight/flight) activation and guide the body back to baseline, achievable in less than ninety seconds.

1. The Figure-Eight Sway. Stand up. Keep your feet planted firmly. Gently sway your hips and upper body in a slow, continuous figure-eight motion. This rhythmic movement is deeply soothing to the vestibular system (your balance sense). Do not focus on anything specific. Just let your body move, slow and low, for ten deep breaths. Rhythmic movement signals stability.

2. The Cold Wrist Splash. Your inner wrists are pulse points where blood vessels run close to the surface. When you feel heat rising (frustration, anger), walk immediately to the sink and splash or hold cold water directly on your wrists for fifteen seconds. This is an immediate, safe shock to the system. It activates the mammalian diving reflex, instantly lowering heart rate and signalling cool-down.

3. The Internal Hum. The Vagus nerve runs down the neck, chest, and diaphragm. Toning this nerve actively promotes calm. When you feel overwhelmed, close your lips and hum loudly, deep in your chest. Feel the vibration behind your sternum and in your throat. Hum for three full exhales. The sound vibration acts like an internal massage for the regulatory system.

4. Heavy Feet Protocol. If you are standing, press your heels down into the floor as hard as you can. Imagine you are trying to sink your entire body weight into the earth below. If you are sitting, plant your feet and press them outward, engaging your leg muscles. This intense grounding provides profound proprioceptive input, anchoring you to the present moment and counteracting the feeling of needing to flee.

5. The Sour Burst. Taste is a powerful, immediate regulatory tool. Keep a tin of intensely sour or minty candies nearby. When anxiety or frustration spikes, pop one into your mouth. The intense, sharp flavor demands the brain's full attention, overriding the emotional spiral. It forces a complete mental reset through the strong sensory input.

6. The Self-Hug Squeeze. Cross your arms over your chest, bringing your hands up to grip the opposite biceps or shoulders. Squeeze gently, then tightly. Hold the tight squeeze for three seconds, then release slightly, maintaining contact. Repeat this squeeze and release five times. This deep pressure provides safe, contained boundaries and triggers the release of oxytocin, a bonding and calming hormone.

7. The 5-4-3-2-1 External Scan. Look around the room. Name out loud: five things you see (e.g., the dust on the shelf, the blue book). Four things you can touch (e.g., the texture of your shirt, the smoothness of the table). Three things you can hear (e.g., the clock ticking, a car outside). Two things you can smell. One thing you can taste (or the taste in your mouth). This forces the prefrontal cortex to engage in simple observation, pulling your focus out of the internal danger narrative.

These are not coping mechanisms; they are physiological tools. They are the quick-access reset button that allows you to move out of instinct and back into intentional, responsive parenting.

—★-★-★—

HOW ALLOWING SMALL FAILURES NOW PREVENTS CRIPPLING PERFECTIONISM AND FEAR OF RISK LATER

Perfectionism is not a pursuit of excellence. It is a shield against shame. It is the anxious nervous system's desperate attempt to control every variable because it perceives mistakes as life-threatening—or at least socially fatal. When a child learns early on that their value or acceptance is tied to flawless performance, they are receiving an instruction manual for chronic anxiety. They stop trying new things. They stop taking risks. They learn to choose avoidance (freeze) over engagement (fight/flight) the moment success is not guaranteed.

As parents, we are terrified of seeing our children struggle. We swoop in quickly. We fix the homework. We call the teacher. We clean up the mess before they even fully register the disappointment. While this feels like love in the moment, it sends a clear, destructive message: "You are not competent enough to handle this disappointment, and I need to keep you safe from discomfort." This robs them of the chance to build a crucial neural pathway: the path of recovery.

True confidence is not knowing you will never fall; it is knowing you can get up when you do. That is competence. Resilience is built in the tiny cracks between effort and result. We must deliberately allow small, supported failures to happen right now, while the stakes are low.

Let them wear the mismatched clothes. Let them forget the minor school project. Let them miscalculate the jump and stumble. When they experience these micro-failures, their nervous system registers a shock, but then quickly observes, "Wait, I failed, and the world did not end. My parent is still here, steady and calm. I survived."

When failure happens, your job shifts entirely. You are not a fixer. You are a steady witness. You regulate yourself first, then offer empathy for their disappointment. "Wow, that feels really frustrating when you spent so much time on it." Wait for them to identify the next step. Do not offer the solution immediately. The key is helping them process the feeling of failure (the nervous system activation) and then empowering them to try a new strategy (the competent action).

The learning is in the recovery, the pivot, and the attempt, not in the initial result. Every small failure they navigate today is an insurance policy against crippling fear of risk tomorrow. We are not aiming for perfect children; we are aiming for capable humans who see mistakes not as indictments of their worth, but as data points on the road to mastery. Give them the space to be imperfect. Give them the gift of their own struggle. It is the foundation of their future strength.

CHAPTER SEVEN

—★-★-★—

EXTERNAL CHAOS, INTERNAL CALM: DEPLOYING YOUR NEW REGULATION SYSTEM AGAINST SCREEN TIME, SOCIAL PRESSURE, AND COMPARISON CULTURE

You have done the deepest work. You have mastered the pause. You have learned to speak peace. You have discovered the hidden wiring of your child's defensive reactions.

Now comes the ultimate test: deploying that internal regulation system against the relentless, amplified, and highly stimulating modern world.

The landscape outside your front door is not built for calm. It is engineered for activation. It is designed to keep the human nervous system in a state of mild, chronic alert. Think about it:

Screen time offers dopamine rushes and flickering light patterns, both immediate stressors.

Social pressure demands conformity and performance, activating deep-seated fear of rejection.

Comparison culture ensures perpetual dissatisfaction, feeding the scarcity mindset that fuels anxiety.

These aren't just abstract worries. These are heavy inputs that constantly flood your child's (and your own) physiological systems. They are stimulants that prevent the Vagus nerve from resting in that gentle, regulated state of connection and peace.

The good news? You cannot stop the world from spinning, but you can build a stable, regulated core within your family that acts like a thermal shield against the external heat. Your primary job now shifts from internal stabilization to mindful environmental engineering.

We are no longer trying to eliminate the chaos—that's impossible. We are learning how to exist within it while remaining internally organized. We are teaching our children how to filter the noise, how to discern what belongs to them, and how to consciously choose calm when the world is demanding panic.

This chapter is about translating your inner calm into external boundaries that protect your family's most precious resource: their peace. We will approach technology, achievement, and social life not through the lens of moral judgment or strict rules, but through the hard science of stimulation management. The question is always: Is this activity serving regulation or driving dysregulation?

When you answer from that place of regulated wisdom, the decisions become astonishingly clear. You stop arguing about arbitrary rules and start protecting physiological safety. And that changes everything.

THE "ANTI-STIMULANT" SCREEN STRATEGY: SETTING TECH BOUNDARIES THAT ACTUALLY REDUCE ANXIETY, NOT JUST CONFLICT

This is perhaps the most charged battlefield in modern parenting. You feel the guilt if you allow too much; you feel the anxiety of the fight when you take it away. We tend to frame screen time as an ethical problem, a failure of willpower, or a sign of laziness. We obsess over the minutes watched and the content consumed.

We need to shift the frame entirely. Technology is not a moral failing; it is a powerful, highly effective nervous system stimulant.

Your child's brain responds to a fast-paced video or a competitive game the same way it responds to being chased by a predator—with high activation. The difference is that instead of activating the fight/flight response via adrenaline, screens deploy the most powerful neurochemical reward system: dopamine.

The fast cuts, the immediate, unpredictable rewards (notifications, likes, winning a round), the bright lights—it's all designed to keep the system slightly activated and highly engaged. It gives the brain what it thinks it wants, rapidly and continuously.

This matters because a child (or an adult) whose nervous system is perpetually over-stimulated cannot transition smoothly, cannot tolerate boredom, and certainly cannot self-regulate when frustrated. The epic meltdown you witness when you enforce a strict boundary isn't a power struggle; it's physiological withdrawal. It's the body screaming because the dopamine drip has suddenly been cut off.

The goal of screen boundaries, therefore, is not to hit a magic number of minutes. The goal is to reduce chronic stimulation and prioritize restorative downtime.

The Anti-Stimulant Strategy redefines boundaries based on regulation, not rules:

1. THE HARD STOP PROTOCOL

Never allow screens immediately before a key transition that requires regulation or connection. This includes thirty minutes before bed, fifteen minutes before family dinner, or directly before homework that requires high focus. Your child cannot go from hyper-activation to deep sleep or intimate connection instantly. They simply cannot. Screens must stop before the body needs to slow down.

2. THE LANDING GEAR TRANSITION

An abrupt cut-off is a shock to the system. You are essentially yanking the plug on their neurological IV drip. We need a transition, a gentle descent, like an airplane deploying its landing gear.

When you announce the five-minute warning, pair it with a physical, sensory regulatory activity that they must start immediately afterward.

For example: "Five more minutes. When the timer goes off, you will put the device in the charging station, and you will spend ten minutes doing big wall push-ups (heavy work) before starting your reading."

This ten-minute transition activity must be non-digital and mildly regulatory. It must be boring enough to allow the nervous system to process the withdrawal, but engaging enough to prevent an immediate outburst. Simple choices include drinking a glass of cold water (sensory input), stretching, listening to quiet instrumental music, or working on a Lego set.

3. THE ENVIRONMENT AUDIT

Screen time often occurs when the child needs to process something difficult or when the parent needs a pause. This is fine, but we must ensure the environment around screen usage is restorative.

Screens should be put away in a central, designated charging station, not carried around or allowed in the bedroom. Bedrooms are for rest, connection, and restorative downtime. When a device is present in a place of rest, it ensures the child remains in a state of anticipatory high alert (waiting for the next notification or impulse).

4. THE SENSORY SWAP FOR DYSREGULATION

If the child is already dysregulated after screen time (crying, irritable, oppositional), do not talk, negotiate, or reason. Their thinking brain (prefrontal cortex) is completely offline. Use sensory input to ground them.

Focus on physical sensations that override the digital buzzing: heavy pressure (a big bear hug or weighted blanket), cold temperatures (holding ice, drinking cold water), or intense physical movement (running outside for one minute). You are giving the body immediate, real, trustworthy information to pull it out of the digital haze.

Remember, the moment you decide that a screen boundary is about protecting your child's nervous system—and your own peace—the conversations become easier. It ceases to be a disciplinary battle and becomes a necessity of health. You are teaching them that sometimes, the most nurturing choice is the quietest one.

—★-★-★—

THE 4 PHRASES YOUR CHILD NEEDS TO HEAR BEFORE A TEST OR SOCIAL EVENT TO FEEL SECURE AND COMPETENT

The contemporary world demands performance from our children earlier and more intensely than ever before. We see the pressure manifest in physical symptoms: stomachaches before the big math test, sudden headaches before the social event. In these moments, your child's nervous system is screaming, "Danger! I am being judged!"

Many parents try to help by saying things like, "Just get an A," or "Don't embarrass me." Even well-intentioned phrases like "You must succeed!" are interpreted by the child's brain as a threat to connection. If they fail, they risk losing your love, or so the primitive brain believes.

Our goal is not to demand excellence, but to offer an internal safety net. Your words must communicate three things: Unconditional acceptance, competence, and a right to regulate.

Here are the four essential messages every child needs to hear before they face external pressure:

1. "I am so proud of the effort you put in. That's what matters most."

This phrase immediately shifts the focus from the outcome (the grade, the perfect social performance) to the process (the study time, the courage to try). Effort is internal and controllable. Results are external and often unpredictable. When you praise effort, you reward hard work and grit. You teach the child that their value is inherent in their commitment, not their achievement. This immediately lowers the intensity of the sympathetic nervous system response because the stakes are no longer tied to external judgment.

2. "If your tummy feels tight or you get stuck, remember to take a deep breath. You can pause."

This is permission to regulate. High-stress situations often trigger the freeze response, causing the child to blank on the test or shut down socially. By acknowledging the physical sensation of anxiety ("tummy feels tight") you validate their internal experience. More importantly, you provide a clear, acceptable exit strategy: the pause. You are teaching them that regulating their body is more important than rushing to an answer. This empowers them to use their own regulatory tools, knowing you approve of the time it takes.

3. "This is just practice. We are doing this so you can learn what you know and what you need next."

The most effective way to combat the pressure of 'The Big Event' is to reframe it. A high-stakes test is rarely truly high stakes. By calling it "practice" or "information gathering," you remove its final, judgmental quality. If a social event goes poorly, it is merely information on how to navigate the next one. This perspective inoculates the child against perfectionism. When they make a mistake, they don't see failure; they see feedback. This cognitive reframe keeps the prefrontal cortex online and accessible, even under pressure.

4. "I trust your brain, and I trust your heart. Go choose the path that feels right for you."

This is the ultimate confidence builder, delivered from a place of regulation. You are ceding control back to the child—the very thing that the regulated adult excels at. You are telling them, explicitly, that they possess the internal resources to handle the situation. "I trust your brain" validates their knowledge and logic. "I trust your heart" validates their intuition and emotional navigation. This phrase is powerful because it allows them to enter the situation with agency, knowing that even if they make a mistake, you support their decision-making process.

By providing these phrases, you are not simply offering encouragement; you are co-regulating their experience, giving them an internal anchor of safety that allows their competence to shine through. You are shifting them from a survival mindset to a thriving mindset.

—★-★-★—

HOW TO BUILD AN INVISIBLE SHIELD AROUND YOUR FAMILY THAT REPELS THE TOXIC COMPARISON TRAP

THE COMPARISON TRAP IS EVERYWHERE. IT IS THE ANXIOUS HUM OF modern life. It feels like a relentless competition. Who has the better car? Whose kid got into the better school? Who schedules the most elite activities?

This constant measuring triggers a chronic state of low-grade threat. It tells your nervous system, and your child's, that your worth is external. That you are only safe if you measure up. This is a profound regulatory burden. It is impossible to feel calm when your value depends on outperforming the person next to you.

The shield is not about isolating your family. It is about defining success internally. It is about creating a thick, protective layer of shared values that cannot be pierced by external metrics.

You must stop measuring the wrong things.

A grade is an achievement. It is an output. It is not a value. A perfect soccer season is an outcome. It is not the measure of integrity.

We need to shift the celebration.

When you focus solely on the achievement, you teach your child that the effort and the character—the parts they can control—are irrelevant compared to the result—the parts they often cannot.

The shield is built on four internal pillars: Effort, Kindness, Curiosity, and Integrity.

Make these your family's currency.

When your child earns an A, celebrate the time they spent studying. Celebrate the perseverance. When they lose a game, celebrate the sportsmanship shown to the opponent. Celebrate their courage for stepping onto the field at all.

This means you must adjust your language.

Stop the immediate, anxious questions about performance. Stop asking, "Did you win? What did you get on the test?"

Start asking: "What did you learn today? Did you feel challenged? Did you help anyone? What made you laugh?"

Create a Family Value Manifesto. Sit down together. Ask your children what makes them feel truly good about themselves. Not proud of an award, but good in their gut. Is it helping a neighbor? Is it finishing a hard book? Is it making their bed without being asked? Write these down. These are your non-negotiables.

When the comparison noise creeps in—and it will—you deploy the shielding talk.

A child says, "Sarah is already reading chapter books and I'm still on easy readers."

Your regulated response is: "That's great for Sarah. We celebrate her joy. But in this family, we measure success by how much we enjoy the journey. Are you curious? Are you trying your best? Then you are winning."

You are validating their observation of the external world, but immediately re-centering them on your family's internal definition of competence.

You are reminding them: We are a safe, steady unit. Our worth is inherent. Our success is measured by the quality of our character, not the size of our portfolio. This consistency is what builds the invisible shield. It allows their nervous system to relax because they know they are loved, not for what they do, but for who they are becoming.

THE SHOCKING HIDDEN COST OF OVER-SCHEDULING: WHY BOREDOM IS THE SINGLE GREATEST TOOL FOR BUILDING RESILIENCE

We are constantly told that the measure of a good parent is how fully they fill their child's calendar. We chase the sports trophies, the musical prodigy moments, the academic advantage. We schedule, we drive, we manage.

We fear that if they aren't doing something productive, they are falling behind.

But this frantic pace is actively sabotaging the resilience we are trying to build.

Consider the human nervous system. It is designed to oscillate between effort and rest. When the effort is relentless, the system remains stuck in a high state of activation. Soccer practice and tutoring are wonderful tools, but when they are stacked back-to-back, the child's brain never gets a moment to process the input. There is no recovery time.

An over-scheduled child is, by definition, an over-activated child. They are running on the energy of perpetual anticipation and performance pressure. They may not melt down at the dinner table, but they are carrying a low-level buzz of chronic stress. This stress is the hidden cost of the perfect calendar.

This is where boredom becomes our single greatest tool.

Boredom is not failure. Boredom is not the absence of activity; it is the presence of an opportunity for the self to show up.

When a child is bored, they are forced to look inward. They must access their own internal resources. They must invent. They must decide. They are activating the parts of their brain responsible for executive function and problem-solving, all without an external deadline or a coach dictating the action.

The ability to create one's own source of engagement is the cornerstone of psychological resilience.

If we constantly provide the entertainment, the instruction, or the next task, we teach them dependence on external input. We train them to require constant stimulation to regulate. This is a path straight to anxiety and screen dependency.

We must create spaciousness.

Spaciousness is the intentional carving out of time that is undefined and unhurried. It is the time where you are simply with your child, not doing something with them.

Genuine connection requires these pauses. It is in the quiet drive, the lazy Sunday afternoon, or the ten minutes after school when nothing is scheduled that the deepest, most authentic conversations often bubble up. These moments signal safety to both your nervous systems. They communicate: We have enough time. We are safe enough to slow down.

If you want to inoculate your child against the pressures of the external world, strip back the calendar. Give them the gift of time. Give them the gift of silence. Give them the profoundly important, restorative, and resilience-building gift of true, unadulterated boredom.

CHAPTER EIGHT

—★-★-★—

THE BLUEPRINT FOR LASTING PEACE: HOW TO INSTALL YOUR NEW NERVOUS SYSTEM HABITS FOR LIFETIME REGULATION

YOU HAVE DONE THE WORK. YOU HAVE IDENTIFIED YOUR TRIGGERS. You have learned the hidden wiring of your own responses. You have practiced the art of the pause. You have repaired the moments of rupture.

This is the final stage. This is where we move from crisis management to sustainable living. We are not just fixing problems anymore; we are building a completely new operating system for your family.

Real, lasting change doesn't come from dramatic, unsustainable overhauls. It comes from tiny, relentless shifts in your daily rhythm. It comes from embedding the awareness of your nervous system into the ordinary moments—the transition from car to kitchen, the waiting for the coffee, the folding of the laundry.

Your body is deeply resistant to novelty. It loves patterns, even dysfunctional ones. To make these new, regulated responses permanent, we must make them easier, more automatic, and less cognitively demanding than the old ones.

Think of it like laying down new railway tracks. At first, the old tracks—the fast, reactive, yelling tracks—look much more worn and tempting. But with consistent, gentle use, the new tracks become the default route.

This chapter is your long-term maintenance plan. It is the blueprint for a life where calm is the baseline, not the exception. It is the promise that the effort you invested will pay off, not just today, but for decades to come.

We shift now from fixing to thriving. We move from surviving to being fully present. This new path is quieter, steadier, and infinitely more joyful. Let's make this peace permanent.

—★-★-★—

THE "AUTOMATIC PILOT" METHOD: WEAVING REGULATION INTO YOUR MORNING COFFEE AND BEDTIME ROUTINE (IT TAKES 2 MINUTES)

Most people fail at self-regulation because they treat it like an intensive, thirty-minute yoga session they must squeeze in. This creates resistance. The Automatic Pilot Method bypasses this resistance by integrating micro-practices into the existing, non-negotiable architecture of your day. We are looking for tiny, consistent touch points that signal safety to your nervous system. Consistency trumps intensity every single time. A focused, two-minute anchor is exponentially more powerful than a missed thirty-minute session.

The key is habit stacking. Find a habit you already perform without thinking—like the coffee brewing, the teeth brushing, or sitting down at the kitchen table—and attach a regulatory moment to it.

MORNING CALIBRATION: THE TWO-MINUTE UPLINK

The goal of the morning practice is to establish a baseline of calm before the demands of the day pull you into reactivity.

1. The Coffee Breath (60 Seconds): While your coffee maker drips or your tea steeps, do not scroll your phone. Instead, stand still. Listen to the sound of the machine. Take three deep, slow breaths that focus only on the

scent of the coffee. Hold the warm mug and notice the warmth spreading through your hands. You are grounding yourself through heat and scent. This is the simplest possible pause.

2. Vertical Alignment (30 Seconds): Before you talk to your child or look at your email, stand up tall. Press your feet firmly into the floor. This is a physical reminder that you are here, now, and stable. A regulated body is one that feels gravity. Notice the sensation of standing.

3. The Mirror Check (30 Seconds): When you are washing your hands or face, look yourself in the eye. Give yourself a genuine, non-judgmental nod. Say internally, "I am here. I am capable." This tiny moment of self-connection anchors your intention for the day.

Evening Discharge: Releasing the Day's Tension

The evening routine is critical for preventing the stresses of the day from spilling into your sleep and contaminating the next morning's starting point.

1. The Toothbrush Anchor (60 Seconds): While brushing your teeth, make the focus purely sensory. Listen to the whir of the brush. Feel the texture of the paste. Focus your eyes on the mirror. This mundane activity becomes a powerful, isolated sensory moment that draws your attention away from mental rumination.

2. Feet on the Floor (60 Seconds): When you first sit or lie down in bed, before you pick up a book or turn on the television, take one full minute to feel the weight of your body pressing into the mattress or the floor. Name three things you are grateful your body did today (e.g., my hands cooked, my legs walked, my voice spoke). This gentle sensory connection signals to the nervous system that the threat is gone and it is safe to rest.

These are not optional extras; they are vital maintenance. By weaving these tiny, consistent moments into the existing tapestry of your life, you are not adding a task—you are upgrading your operating system. The automatic pilot is built on repetition. Do the small thing reliably, and the large shift in your overall peace will follow. Your regulation system will start running quietly in the background, ready to support you when the chaos inevitably knocks.

—★-★-★—

WARNING: THE SECRET TRAP OF THINKING YOU MUST DO THIS ALONE (AND WHEN TO CALL IN THE REGULATION EXPERTS)

THIS IS THE SECRET THAT KEEPS MANY BRILLIANT, LOVING PARENTS trapped in endless cycles of struggle: the belief that they must be the sole architects of their family's emotional regulation.

We are taught, implicitly or explicitly, that asking for help with parenting is a confession of failure. You bought the book, you learned the science, so why are you still snapping? Why isn't the calm holding?

The truth is simple: You are dealing with systems that have years, sometimes decades, of ingrained defensive programming. Sometimes the historical trauma, the deep-seated fears, or the chemical imbalances in the brain are too entrenched for self-help alone.

We need to normalize support. We need to reframe seeking professional help not as a sign of defeat, but as a commitment to excellence. You are commissioning a specialist to help overhaul the foundational wiring of your family's emotional infrastructure. That is strategic. That is brave.

WHEN DO YOU CALL IN THE REGULATION EXPERTS?

YOUR REGULATION TOOLKIT IS DESIGNED TO MANAGE THE DAILY friction of family life. But there are specific thresholds where specialized intervention becomes essential for safety and lasting change.

1. Functional Impairment: If your family's stress is regularly interfering with daily life—sleep, school attendance, friendships, or your ability to

function at work—it's time for outside help. If the anxiety is so intense that it prevents the child from attempting new things or causes severe physical symptoms (headaches, stomach aches), seek consultation immediately.

2. Intensity and Persistence: You have been consistently applying the regulation tools for weeks, and the intensity or frequency of the dysregulation (either yours or your child's) is not decreasing. If your child's emotional reactions feel bigger, scarier, or more frequent than what is typical for their age, that persistent red zone activation needs expert guidance.

3. The Parent is Running on Empty: If you, the parent, feel perpetually depleted, emotionally numb, or are relying on coping mechanisms that are starting to harm you (excessive drinking, isolating yourself), it is time to seek your own trauma-informed therapist. Remember, a regulated adult is the prerequisite. If your tank is empty, no amount of technique will work.

4. Concerning Behaviors: Any behavior that crosses into the territory of self-harm, suicidal ideation, severe aggression toward others, or a sudden, drastic regression in developmental milestones requires immediate professional assessment. This is not a parenting problem; this is a nervous system emergency.

What Kind of Expert?

You aren't looking for just any therapist. You are looking for a regulation expert. These are often therapists who specialize in somatic (body-based) practices, trauma-informed care, and specific modalities like Polyvagal Theory, EMDR, or brainspotting. For children, look for play therapists, expressive arts therapists, or pediatric behavioral specialists who understand that behavior is communication, not defiance.

Reaching out for support is not a detour on your path toward peace; it is often the shortest, most direct route. It is the moment you stop carrying the crushing weight of the entire emotional landscape and allow someone to share the load.

There is no shame in requiring specialized assistance to heal wounds that were often inflicted long before your child was born. Your decision to call for help protects the peace you have worked so hard to cultivate. It secures the legacy of regulation you are building for your family.

—★-★-★—

YOUR REWIRED INTUITION: HOW A CALMER NERVOUS SYSTEM MAKES YOU THE SMARTEST, MOST TRUSTWORTHY PARENT IN THE ROOM

FOR SO LONG, YOU WERE FORCED TO OUTSOURCE YOUR WISDOM.

You bought the books. You joined the forums. You frantically Googled every rash, every defiant stare, every sigh of your teenager. Every parenting moment felt like a high-stakes final exam, and you were desperately searching for the answer key somewhere outside of yourself.

Why?

Because anxiety is loud. Fear is an insistent, demanding alarm bell that screams, "DANGER! ACT NOW!" This alarm—the dysregulated nervous system—drowns out the quiet, consistent hum of your true parental intuition. You couldn't hear yourself think, let alone trust yourself to lead.

Now, things are different.

You have consistently chosen the pause. You have anchored yourself in the ventral vagal state. You have built a steady foundation. What happens when the alarm is finally silenced?

Your intuition comes online.

The intuition that emerges from a regulated state is not the same as the impulse that springs from fear. Fear-based impulse says: Control them. Yell louder. Punish them so they learn. Regulated intuition says: Slow down. Look closer. Their distress is not a threat; it is a signal.

This is why a regulated adult is the smartest parent in the room. Not because you have memorized more child psychology terms, but because you are accessing the deepest, clearest part of your own intelligence.

When you are calm, the answers flow.

You know instinctively when to push and when to back off. You know exactly what kind of boundary your strong-willed child needs versus the boundary your sensitive child needs. You understand immediately that the tantrum is rooted in fatigue, not defiance. This isn't a magical gift; it is the natural efficiency of a nervous system that is not wasting energy scanning for danger.

Trust the quiet guidance you have uncovered.

Your inner voice is no longer distorted by panic. It is steady, specific, and trustworthy. Stop searching for the guru on the outside. You are the expert. You are the safe haven. Your calm is the compass.

This ability to sense, rather than guess, is the ultimate reward of nervous system work. It is the final shift that moves you from reacting to responding, and from perpetual self-doubt to unshakable confidence. You have become the trustworthy leader your children always knew you could be.

—★-★-★—

THE MULTI-GENERATIONAL BENEFIT: HOW YOUR DECISION TODAY CHANGES THE EMOTIONAL DESTINY OF YOUR GRANDCHILDREN

WE OFTEN FOCUS ON THE IMMEDIATE. THE FRANTIC ENERGY OF THE present moment. Did I handle the homework meltdown correctly? Did I set the boundary firmly enough?

But the shift you have made is not a temporary fix. It is a generational change agent.

You are not merely regulating your children. You are closing a circuit breaker on inherited anxiety. You are deciding that the stress responses passed down from your parents, and perhaps from theirs—the quick tempers, the silent shutdowns, the chronic worry—stop here. They stop with you.

The greatest gift you can pass on is not college tuition or a family heirloom. It is a stable nervous system.

Your children are internalizing your regulated presence as the default setting for family life. They watch you pause before you react. They observe you name your frustration without unleashing it. They see you repair the connection after a moment of rupture.

This is the ultimate training in emotional intelligence. This is how resilience is built, brick by breath.

When they leave home, they will carry not a sack full of rules, but an internal blueprint for handling stress. They will understand that high emotions do not equal emergency. They will know that safety is something they can create within their own bodies, not something dependent on external perfection.

Imagine your grandchildren.

They will be raised by adults who know how to access their own calm. They will witness parents who communicate limits with compassion and who normalize strong feelings. The quiet, steady effort you put into regulating your own reactions today means your grandchildren will grow up with less inherited trauma to untangle. They will start their lives operating from a baseline of security, not scarcity.

You are giving them a foundation of emotional tolerance. You are ensuring that their home, built by your children, is defined by empathy and genuine connection.

You stepped off the default path of reactive living. You chose to feel the discomfort, to do the hard internal work. That choice is a monumental gift. It is the legacy of quiet strength. It is the promise of emotional peace for generations yet to come. You have changed their destiny.

AFTERWORD

THE ONLY THING YOU NEED TO REMEMBER WHEN CHAOS NEXT KNOCKS (VALUE: $1,997 IN THERAPY)

You made it.

You walked through the chaos. And you found the stillness within it.

Remember, the goal was never perfection.

It was presence.

It was becoming the regulated adult who understands that true strength lies in softness.

Thank you for trusting me with this journey.

Now go breathe.

And enjoy the calm you have earned.

www.ingramcontent.com/pod-product-compliance
Lightning Source LLC
La Vergne TN
LVHW051044210926
848486LV00001B/11